Thriving as a ~~Single Mom, Raising~~ Happy Kids

Support for Mothers Who Are Parenting Solo

Copyright 2024
Chistell Publishing
https://www.chistell.com
First Printing, February 2024

All rights reserved

Published by: Chistell Publishing
               7235 Aventine Way, Suite #201
               Chattanooga, TN 37421

Author: Denise Turney
ISBN: 979-8-9856651-5-4

Dedication

For my son.

I love you, Gregory –

Table of Contents

Chapter 1 – You're Someone's "Mom!" — 10
- Celebrate New Birth — 14
- No Greater Role in This World — 19
- The Journey Here — 22

Chapter 2 – You Can Do This — 24
- Looking Within — 26
- What You're Really Made With — 29
- See The Wins — 31

Chapter 3 – Like an Artist — 33
- Shaping a Beautiful Life — 35
- Focus on the Goal — 39
- Your Child's True Nature — 41
- Start Early — 44
- Be Consistent — 47

Chapter 4 – A Personal Journey — 49
- No Better Mom — 51
- An Uninterrupted Path — 53
- Witness — 58

Chapter 5 – Trust the Process	**60**
Force Free Living	62
About School	65
Put Yourself on Time-Out	70
Chapter 6 – Relationships	**74**
Leaving Bad Relationships in the Past	80
Introducing Your Child to New People	82
Keeping Your Child Safe	85
Getting Love	89
Chapter 7 – Managing Money	**93**
Reducing Debt	95
Growing Savings	99
Financial Support	102
Chapter 8 – Balancing Work	**106**
Childcare	109
Set Clear Work Timelines	111
Powerful Communication	114
Be Disciplined	117

Chapter 9 – Strong Support	**119**
Family Near and Far	122
Circle of Friends	124
Worship Centers	127
Volunteer	130
Chapter 10 – When It Gets Hard	**132**
Get Still	134
Call Your Sister	137
Pray and Trust	140
Talk to Another Single Mother	142
Journaling Helps	144
Chapter 11 – What About You	**146**
Design Your Beautiful Life	148
Opening Your Heart	150
Fun is Part of Thriving	154
Three Things	156
Chapter 12 – Shifts and Changes	**159**
Childhood to Adulthood – So Much Change	161
Unexpected Experiences	163

Watching a Human Bloom	165
Patience Matters	168
Chapter 13 – Growing Up Happy	**172**
Play is a Great Teacher	174
You Are "Mama"	176
More About Timeout	179
Precious Memories	181
Chapter 14 – Letting Go	**185**
Growing into Independence	187
Decision Makers	189
Being There	191
Happy Kids	193
Chapter 15 – Thrive	**195**
Next Steps	197
Welcome New Changes	199
You're a Champion!	201
Empowering Single Mom Quotes	203
Journal Pages	211
References	**229**
Resources	**230**

"Love is the most powerful link between you and your child."

Thriving as a Single Mom While Raising Happy Kids

Congratulations on becoming a mom! You're part of a miracle, a tremendous blessing! Get ready for an amazing journey! You're about to learn a lot about yourself and your child. If you allow it, your world will open wide – in incredibly good ways.

Everything you've felt before will be magnified. If you've felt surprised before, prepare for instances when you'll feel shocked. If you've felt happiness, going forward there will be experiences that fill you up with joy. Fun shifts into excitement. And more times than you might be able to count tired turns into exhaustion.

Although you can parent on your own, to parent effectively, you need support. Within the pages of this book are insights, researched material, resources, tips, guidance, and shared single mom experiences that I wish I'd had while I was raising my child alone.

Back then, I longed for someone to talk with about single mom challenges, someone who was walking the path I was on. Whether I was struggling to quieten my colicky son, make rent, secure a better salaried job, date again or help my son with schoolwork, I wished that I had someone to get advice and support from.

Years ago, I was truly a single mom, living 500 miles from my nearest relative. My mom had transitioned when I was seven years old, so I didn't have my mom to lean for support as I raised my son. Fortunately, my son's father was active in his life.

Another blessing is that I'd watched my father raise me and my four siblings as a single parent. That, combined with my faith in the Creator, is where I gained the deep belief that I could parent solo successfully. My childhood is also where I learned a lot of effective parenting skills.

Building a support system was key to parenting successfully as a single mom for me. Single parenting is no time to be an island, a topic covered in <u>Thriving as a Single Mom While Raising Happy Kids</u>. Financial, mentoring, tutoring, co-parenting, etc. resources are also shared within these pages as are many other key events and experiences you might face as a single parent -- experiences like raising a joyous, balanced child, paying down debt and growing savings, fulfilling your personal dreams, keeping your child safe, dealing with life after your child becomes an adult and more.

Although this book is not a medical or professional guidebook, it's a valuable supportive tool. Should you or your child need professional or medical assistance, please seek help from a licensed professional.

Regarding single parenting, much is learned through experience – trial and error – hard lessons. Years passed before I learned a lot that's covered in <u>Thriving as a Single Mom While Raising Happy Kids.</u> In fact, I learned a lot of what's shared within the pages of this book the hard way. You don't have to.

It is my sincere hope that <u>Thriving as a Single Mom While Raising Happy Kids</u> makes the amazing journey you're undertaking easier and increasingly rewarding. Gain the most from this book.

Here's to you and your child!

"Your child's birth changes everything. Just as your birth changed everything."

Chapter 1 – You're Someone's "Mom!"

Welcome to a world of wonder! You might not see it now, but your entire life is changing, starting with your name!

Until now, you answered to several names – your birth name, a shortened version of your birth name, and a nickname or two. Even more, since you graced this world with your magnificent presence, you may have been called - daughter, sister, niece, aunt, cousin, wife, and friend. That's all changing! From here on, to your blessed child, you are an amazing "Mom!"

I remember when my son's paternal grandmother told me, late in my third trimester, "Soon you'll be 'Mom' to someone!" Those words still resonate.

Over the years, especially when my son was a child, I was called "Mom" more times than I can count. "Mom, can I go outside and play?" "Mom, are we going to the toy store today?" "Mom, my stomach hurts." "Mom, what's for dinner?" "Mom, can I stay up late?" "Mom, will you go to the park with me?"

Another human being, an infant small enough to fit in your hands, loves you, adores you, reveres you – treasures you. This small infant also depends on you and has an unspoken confidence and trust that you will come through, time after time.

You've become a mom! This shift is too great, too vast, and amazing to describe. *It must be experienced.* Howbeit and as fulfilling and rewarding as motherhood is, the journey of single motherhood calls for faith and uncommon inner strength, because you're taking the journey of raising a human being on your own.

It's not an easy task – and it will definitely have ups and downs, offering countless opportunities to learn and grow -- which is why your friends, parents and other relatives might have told you that being a single parent is hard. A few people you know might have warned you that life as a single mom is *too* hard.

But I'm here to tell you that you can parent effectively; you can parent with success! Regardless of the path that led to you being a single parent – divorce, your child's father transitioning, never marrying, adopting, widowhood, raising the child of a friend or sibling who has transitioned – you have the inner resources to parent successfully. You can raise a happy, healthy child, someone who grows into a responsible, happy, loving adult.

My son was five years old when I filed for divorce and became a single mom. I can still remember hearing inner guidance tell me that raising my son alone was going to be hard.

What I didn't hear was that it was *impossible*. As if it had happened to fill me with *good strength*, I also had the memory of my father raising me and my four siblings on his own after my mom transitioned and, years later, after my stepmother and father divorced.

Thanks to my dad, I *really* knew that I could raise a child on my own and do it exceptionally well. I also knew to trust my Creator (Proverbs 3:5). On top of that, there were a myriad of women who were raising kids on their own. But I had a son to raise, and, for some reason, I thought raising him would be harder than raising a girl.

To tell you bringing my son up was easy would be a lie. To tell you that it was the most rewarding thing I've done in this world would be an immense understatement.

Over the years, my son and I became deeply connected in a healthy non-codependent way. When my son was a kid, we had fun together. *Kenan & Kel*, *The Rugrats* and *Hey Arnold!* were among the favorite TV shows that we watched together and, I'm telling you, I enjoyed watching those shows as much as my son, Gregory, did!

We cheered for Allen Iverson and the Philadelphia 76ers like cheering was going out of style. When my son was younger, no older than five years old, we went to the park together. I'd sit on a swing and watch Gregory go up and down the sliding board.

Come dusk, my son would jump on his big wheel with his neighborhood friends. He'd pedal fast and furiously around the apartment buildings. Around and around he and his friends would go. Did they ever have fun!

Then, there were the times when we'd cook together. When he was a kid, my son loved meatloaf. Later it was baked chicken, fish, and organic food. He trusted me and I trusted him. Communicating with each other came easily. For me, there are no sweeter memories than the years I raised my son as a single mom.

Sweet memories await you too. Share your love with your child and you could create a bond that nothing can break. When your child is grown, after you've done so much good work, your child and you might become good-good friends.

The laughter, fun and learning will continue. So too will misunderstandings and miscommunication. But you'll always love each other. This is your chance to get an incredibly important relationship right. And you can! You're someone's mom now.

Celebrate New Birth

It's time to celebrate! Celebrate the birth of your child, a new life that's a part of you, a new life you'll imprint your loving influence upon. Come on! Celebrate!

Looking for ideas? Treat yourself to your favorite meal of vegetables, fruit, and pasta or maybe you prefer seafood or another delicious dish.

Graciously accept invitations from family and friends to let them pamper you with care, affection, and support. If you know someone who's genuinely trustworthy and psychologically healthy and they offer to watch your newborn for a few hours at your home, allowing you to sleep, consider accepting the offer. During the coming days and nights, you'll be glad that you did.

Take lots of pictures of your newborn as well as plenty of pictures of you holding your baby. Enjoy gifts you receive from visitors who stop by to see you and your child; enjoy receiving these gifts free of an ounce of guilt.

If you're alone, gift yourself with days relaxing while your child is quiet. Read a book, listen to music or watch a movie you appreciate. Talk on the phone with a friend. Soak in a bubble bath. Assure yourself that, just because you're alone, in an environment where there's just your child and you, blessings approach and you're always loved and cared for.

Just as you did while you were carrying your child, you're creating precious memories. Consider capturing them in a photo album, a journal and with video. There's a lot of living ahead for your child and you. Memories that you create now can be shared and cherished by you and your child, especially after your child becomes an adult.

As tempting as it may be to try to see the end from the beginning, live free of worrying about the future or the past. As Isaiah 43:18 shares, "Forget the former things; do not dwell on the past."

Newness has come. Days will fill up with excitement, chores, baby cries, cooing, playfulness, work, paying bills, trips to and from the babysitter or daycare and fun.

During times of restlessness or intense sleepiness, remind yourself that moments of wonder are ahead. Live in the present. For now, and during each coming day, remind yourself to celebrate what you're experiencing.

After all, being a single mom has a special effect on the perception of time. Although each single mom is different, it's as if time slows down when your child is young.

There is so much to attend to: late night feedings, holding your baby, playing with your little one, changing diapers, washing laundry, exploring with your child, letting your child know that they are loved. Before you know it, you're focusing on what you're doing *now* with your baby. And living in the present becomes easier, natural. That alone is worth celebrating!

Celebrate What You're Experiencing Now

(*Use the below space to capture feelings, baby firsts, etc. Add pictures too!*)

_____

_____

_____

_____

_____

_____

_____

_____

Pictures Say So Much!

No Greater Role in this World

As a single mom you may fulfill one of the world's greatest roles. Why? You are about to influence a human life in a way that, perhaps, no one else can – other than another mom. If you live alone, you'll be the strongest influence on your child.

To your child, you are a heroine. In fact, you're the most important person in the world to your infant. For this and other reasons, make time you spend with your child a priority.

Accept that your life has changed and will continue to change, more with each passing day, in good, enriching ways *if* you make and follow through on the right choices. During tough times, ask a single mom whose children are adults how much she misses the days when her children were young, how much fun they had during holidays and "regular" days.

Revisit your childhood to discover traditions and child rearing techniques your parents shared with you, experiences you appreciate. Which, if any, of these traditions and techniques do you want to bring into your child's life?

_____

_____

_____

_____

_____

As the greatest role model in your child's world, make good use of inner vision. For example, how do you want to raise your child? Do you want to:

- Raise your child in a diverse environment, teaching your child two to three languages
- Educate your child in a religious belief
- Teach your child to respect nature and all living beings
- Lead your child into a life of independence
- Empower your child with self-love
- Encourage your child to develop strong, healthy social skills
- Hone your child's creative abilities
- Push your child toward a certain career
- Motivate your child toward physical fitness and a lifelong healthy diet
- Make earning good grades in school a priority
- Honor the importance of family and respecting ancestors

Additionally, are there mistakes your parents made while raising you that you want to avoid? Which ones and why?

As you observe your child, watching her natural tendencies, what easily gains his attention, focus on ways to teach tenderness, sharing, caring, trust and honesty. Support your child's inherent inclinations. Allow your child to bloom into the person they are meant to be. You could achieve this by:

- Giving your child room to explore in safe ways free of input from you
- Allow your child to pick out games they want to play

- Encourage your child to engage in creative arts
- Let your child have fun playing with other kids
- Ask your child to share toys
- Gift your child with the freedom to make mistakes without being disciplined or ridiculed

Also, step into the single mom role with confidence. Just because this might be the first time you're raising a child doesn't mean that you don't already have the foundational skills to parent successfully.

Tip: Prayer, meditation, quiet walks in nature and stillness (sitting on the porch, a stoop, swing, chair or sofa) can do wonders should you start to feel as if the role of "single mom" is filled with too much overwhelm. Seek guidance from the Creator and trust the process of parenting your child.

The Journey Here

You may have arrived at this juncture on the single motherhood journey for one or more reasons and while traveling down different paths, years of twists and turns. There's no other mother like you. It's a fact that each single mom is different. And each single mom's journey is different.

Divorce set me on the path to single motherhood. My son was five-years-old when his father and I divorced. Although she was married, my grandmother grew up at a time when women were deemed to be the sole caretakers of the children in the family. She and my paternal grandfather were married for 60 years, but my grandmother did most of the heavy lifting when it came to caring for their three children.

Perhaps you never married your child's father. Or you might have been married and due to an accident or another unfortunate event, you became widowed.

Early courtship days with your child's father might have been filled with trust, warmth and great expectation. Once you discovered that you were pregnant, both you and your child's father might have exhibited a myriad of emotions, including joy, excitement, tremendous hope, worry, fear, confusion, and peace.

Since you learned that you were pregnant, emotions you've felt have likely rocked and swayed and changed. You might have doubted that you can parent a child successfully by yourself. This bears repeating -- You can.

Don't get caught up in the journey that you took to become a single mom. However, you became a single mom, you're now in one of the world's most powerful roles.

You and your child need your courage, your inner vision, your guidance and your love. It's also important to remember that it's not just your child's life that you're impacting, you're impacting and changing your own life. Make this journey good.

What 3 Things Do You Appreciate About Motherhood?

1. _____

2. _____

3. _____

"You're stronger than you think."

Chapter 2 – You Can Do This

How many experiences have you faced and overcome that you thought you couldn't deal with? Look back over your time in this world and recall specific events, including how certain you were that you were unable to succeed at what you needed to do.

Recall how you created a plan of action and took the necessary steps to get through what you faced. Let yourself feel emotions that you felt then, especially the exhilarating emotion of success as you met, perhaps even exceeded, the tasks.

You're about to do it again. You really are.

There's support, practices, and choices you can incorporate into your day to make parenting easier. As you continue, you'll get stronger, smarter – wiser.

Should you feel uncertain about your ability to parent successfully, here are options you could take:

- Read memoirs and autobiographies of women who raised a child to be a responsible, loving, well-balanced and happy adult.
- Join a support group for single moms. Allow yourself to be empowered as you listen to other women who are raising their children alone share their challenges and triumphs.

- Read articles about entrepreneurs, scientists, inventors, community leaders, athletes, worship center leaders, educators, etc. who were raised by a single mom.

- Invest in a support system. This is a group of trustworthy people who you can talk with when you're feeling overwhelmed. People who make up your support system might help babysit, visit you, chat, listen to the latest album by your favorite singer or watch a good movie and laugh with you.

To stay strong, you need to be aware of how you're feeling. You also need to *be honest with yourself* about how you're feeling. For example, if you've been unusually impatient or short-tempered, consider taking a day off from work.

If your child's father is mentally and emotionally healthy and active in your child's life, do something fun while your child is with him. As tempting as it might be, avoid filling up all slow times with volunteer work, chores, projects or office work.

You'll feel open, refreshed, and strong if you schedule breaks into your week. These breaks could be as short as 30 minutes or as long as four hours. Strength means you don't push yourself too much, take on too many responsibilities or consistently burden yourself. You need and deserve time to rest, have fun and relax. It's a part of being strong.

Looking Within

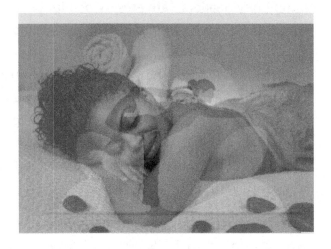

Have you watched the news for an hour? If so, did watching the news make you feel hopeful, happy, and energized? Or did you feel concerned, powerless, and frustrated – maybe even angry as you listened to stories about crime, political unrest, weather storms and economic shifts?

Focus on what's happening in the outer world (e.g., news) and don't be surprised if your mood, belief in good and overall well-being drops. Even more, if you focus on upcoming job projects, someone you've been bumping heads with or a bill you need to pay a week from now, you won't feel your best.

Investing time in watching the news isn't the only way to pull yourself down. Repetitively thinking about how your child is performing in school, the long commute to and from work, and bills you need to pay are other ways to ensure you don't feel your best.

As tempting as it is to believe otherwise, living an optimal life doesn't come from outside of you. The strength of an empowering mindset shows up when you look within.

Pay attention to- what's happening in your inner world. Are the thoughts you have about your children caring and kind? Do you invest in a diet that keeps you well fueled and healthy? Is it common for you to think loving thoughts about yourself?

What do you see and feel when you look within?

If you see and hear self-judgment, criticism, or put-downs, change your inner scripts. See yourself as your best friend. And start thinking about yourself that way. As a tip, you could speak the below messages to yourself when you wake and before drifting to sleep:

- Each day, in each and every way, I'm getting better.
- I'm a perfect creation, forever loved, forever loving.
- Within me is an unending strength that gets me through anything I face.
- I love myself and I am learning to love myself more deeply.
- My parenting skills improve each and every day, helping me to raise a beautiful, powerful, peaceful, responsible and loving human being.

Feel free to add to the list! And remember, you're already repeating messages (scripts) to yourself. If you don't think so, it's because you're repeating the scripts within your subconscious mind, making the effects of the scripts powerful. Today, take control of the scripts – creating and repeating messages that empower you.

Why is this so important? Effective parenting requires good energy. It calls for courage, confidence, and solid self-respect.

Also, whether you realize it or not, you'll project the way you feel about yourself onto your children. So, take breaks, utilize your support system, and speak love to yourself.

What You're Really Made With

It's true. Single parenting is hard. In fact, there are times when it feels like you're bound to fail, but you aren't. You really can parent a child into a healthy, loving, responsible adult.

And it's not just because you're capable of caring for another human. You're an eternal being, someone who can face fear, look it down and meet great challenges.

You're a winner. You were created to succeed.

Get this into your thought system. Really grab hold of it. Believe it because it's true. (Note: *Repetition gets thoughts into your subconscious, so this truth will be repeated throughout this book.*)

Another reason to believe in your innate goodness is that you're going to need this belief to do what you must do. In fact, you'll only go as far as your beliefs allow.

If you believe in the Creator or a Higher Power and that the Higher Power created you to be like it, that alone should reveal what you're really made with. Even if you don't believe it yet, you can face any challenge. Millions of moms already have, and so can you.

Reading scriptures like Genesis 1:31 can open you up to the truth of what you are. Accept truths about yourself.

Also, accepting what you're *really* made of isn't a one-time thing. When raising a child as a single mom gets "painfully tough" remind yourself of what you're made with.

The older your child becomes, the easier this might get. Regardless of what transpires, and even if others judge your parenting skills harshly (especially as you start parenting for the first time), don't diminish your worth. Instead, remind yourself of what you are created to be.

List 5 Things You Love About Yourself!

See The Wins

See yourself being understanding with your child, especially during times when your child pushes your patience (e.g., in-store tantrums, getting creative in the living room with a can of bright red paint you forgot to seal the lid on). Also, see yourself supporting your child's spiritual, physical, academic, social, mental, and emotional growth.

People who have experienced exceptional success have shared that one or more of their parents saw their success early and mapped out plans to get them on the right path. What you see happening to you and your child matters. Therefore, while bathing or showering, spend 60 to 90 seconds visualizing yourself parenting effectively.

Don't stop there. See your child becoming more confident and taking smart risks, the type of risks that pay off over the short and long-term.

Let this serve as a guide. Even if your family has one or more members who have made mistakes that got them expelled from school or, worse, forced to deal with law enforcement, steer clear of expecting the same for your children. What happened in your family before does not have to repeat itself.

Stay clear of thinking that the best you can do as a parent is to raise a child who stays out of jail or prison. That's aiming too low (way too low). So too is expecting your child to make the same mistakes that you or their father made.

Don't do that. Instead, see the wins.

See yourself winning at parenting. See your child winning as they grow and develop. See yourself becoming the first person in your family to fulfill her dreams whether that's owning a profitable business, earning a college degree, paying off a mortgage a decade early, leading a team at work, pursuing an art, mentoring, or serving at a worship center.

When you look to the future or consider what you can do right now, see the wins. Doing so is as easy as seeing yourself failing (*something you may have been doing for far too long*).

Use your imagination and start to see yourself succeeding at parenting and other things you want to do. Later in <u>Thriving While Raising Happy Kids as a Single Mom</u>, we'll discuss actions you can take to achieve goals that are important to you.

"Create a Masterpiece."

Chapter 3 – Like an Artist

There may be nothing more beautiful than a life well lived. Now that you're a mom, not only can you create a masterpiece of your life, but you can create a masterpiece of your child's life through the parenting you do.

Consider approaching single parenting like an artist. Realize the impact of what you say to your child. Accept the influence your mood has on your child.

Even before your child is old enough to understand words, they pick up your energy. In fact, Psych Central shares that, "Babies who are already born can experience rejection from a mother. There are decades of research on **attachment bonds** that help explain this." Furthermore, "Too much stress over the long term can pose challenges via the release of stress hormones, like cortisol, into the amniotic fluid."[1]

Parent in a way that shows you know how much each comment, suggestion, double take, raised eyebrow, embrace and pat on the back means to your child. When your child makes a mistake, if you speak in an unloving or threatening manner, catch yourself. Pivot and redirect your language and behavior.

These self-checks and pivots might seem small, but they add up. In fact, one to two encouraging words a day could build your child's confidence the same as one to two criticisms from you to your child each day could erode your child's confidence.

Parent as if you're an artist with an easel filled with different paints and a blank canvas. What you say and do as your child's parent helps to create your child's personality. What you say and do will show up in your child's life, perhaps for years.

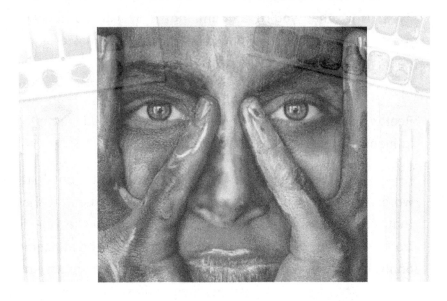

Shaping a Beautiful Life

Your newborn will experience a massive amount of development, similar to how your child experienced a great deal of change as an embryo. Because of this, you have the power to shape a beautiful life.

If you don't think so, check out these research findings. For starters and as shared in *Business Insider*, "Countless studies and extensive clinical research have found links between your parents' behavior during childhood and how you act as an adult."[2]

More specifically, "If your parents spoke negatively about their bodies, you are more likely to have low self confidence." And "If your parents told you white lies, it may have led you to have issues trusting others in adulthood."[2]

Regarding childhood development, you can build healthy attachment with your child, enriching her development. The impact of the attachment bond cannot be overstated. In fact, Help Guide shares that, "Since the quality of the attachment bond profoundly impacts your child's development, experiencing attachment issues can affect their ability to express emotions, build resilience, trust, and confidence, and enjoy healthy relationships. Some studies show that insecure attachment can even contribute to behavioral problems, such as bullying."[3]

If you made attachment mistakes, there's good news. "No matter how detached or insecure your child seems, or how frustrated or exhausted you feel from trying to connect with them, it is possible to repair an attachment issue," according to Help Guide.

Whether you want to keep getting parenting right or need to repair a mistake you made, break the work of childrearing into small steps. This approach could reduce the times when parenting on your own feels like "too huge" a job. For instance, instead of thinking of parenting your child from toddler to adult, focus on parenting day-to-day or week-to-week.

Activities that you engage in over a day could expand as the week goes on. This is another reason why it's important to break your parenting "to-dos" down. Here are activities that you might fulfill as a single mom:

- Wash, dry, fold and put away baby clothes
- Prepare baby food/meals
- Bathe your child
- Read to your child
- Clean your home
- Drive your child to daycare / babysitter's
- Commute to and from work (if you work outside home)
- Clean baby bottles
- Breast feed your child
- Weave baskets for your child to sleep in
- Wash cloth baby wrapping carriers
- Grocery shop
- Exercise
- Purchase diapers
- Shop for infant clothes

- Dress yourself and your child
- Work (if you work remotely or outside your home)
- Tend to your child's cries (changing diapers, burping, etc.)

That's just a start. When your child is old enough to attend school, the list will certainly change, likely getting longer. After your child starts school, regular action items might include:

- Drive your child to school
- Commute to and from work
- Check school homework
- Make sure your child is safe while they play outside with friends
- Spend quality time with your child (reading with your child, playing a game with your child, talking with your child without interruptions or being distracted, etc.)
- Prepare a meal
- Travel to retrieve water from a faraway well (depending on where you live in the world)
- Plant seeds, till the land and gather harvests
- Wash dishes
- Clean your home
- Exercise
- Pay bills
- Review and sign required school forms
- Grocery shop
- Work (if you work remotely or outside your home)
- Pick child up from school and drive home
- Homeschool your child

- Drive child to sports / after school events
- Attend PTA meetings
- Supervise how much TV your child watches
- Set a limit on how much time your child spends online
- Attend child's school performances
- Volunteer as a chaperone at school events

Although it's tempting to review the list of responsibilities you need to deal with while you lay in bed at night, try not to do this. After all, you've already filled an entire day with activity.

Now that you're in bed, it's time to rest and allow your body, including your brain, the opportunity to rest and recharge. If you don't allow your whole being to rest and recharge each night, you could be on your way to feeling overwhelmed. Let this happen and you'll have no choice but to take a break.

A better option than thinking about your entire next day's activities is to wait until morning to think about the first activity you'll complete. This way, you'll train your brain to expect to rest in the evenings.

Good rest allows you to recharge. And rest is not only physical. To fully rest, you need to relax your mind and not worry about the future. Being rested and recharged helps boost your mood; it also keeps you in a good vibration which benefits you and your child.

Focus on the Goal

Just as rest is key to effective parenting, so too is focusing on the goal. The ultimate goal is to guide and parent your child into a resilient, healthy, joy-filled adult. After you've done your work, your child should feel confident, well-balanced, ready to spread their wings and start mapping out their personal journey.

Focusing on the ultimate goal will influence your decisions, both in the moment and across an entire day. For instance, if you want your child to have confidence, you'll encourage your child when they make a mistake, bring home a poor grade, or submit to a bullying figure. You'll encourage your child without comparing them to anyone else, including a sibling.

Regarding the power of focus, check out these researched findings on what focusing can help you achieve. To start, parental focus requires you to pay attention to positives. Here's what the Center for Parenting Education shares about this type of focus, "Ask yourself what kind of people you want your children to become, and then consider what you can do to model the behaviors and attitudes that would reflect that kind of person. This is another way of saying that it is helpful for you to examine your own values."[4]

Child Focus has this to say about parental focus, "The attention we give our children plays a monumental role in determining how they will grow and develop."[5] Additionally, Child Mind Institute says, "The idea is that for children, parental attention is so powerful that whatever behavior we pay attention to will increase, even if we're telling them to stop."[6]

Unless you've mastered quieting your mind, you're likely to focus on an event, topic or memory throughout the day and night - something. And sure. What you focus on changes. What doesn't change is the power of your focus.

What do you focus on when imagining your child's future?

1. _____

2. _____

3. _____

4. _____

5. _____

Your Child's True Nature

By the time your child reaches middle school, it might surprise you how similar your child's personality, beliefs, and habits are to yours. You'll also be surprised, maybe even shocked, at how different your child is from you.

The differences could indicate that you allowed your child to develop into who they truly are. Differences could show that you didn't force your child to deny or repress anything about their true nature.

For me, when I was a kid, that freedom came in the form of my dad allowing me to read loads of books, visit the library on my own and spend late nights banging out a novel on a noisy blue manual typewriter. Reading a lot of books, going to the library, and writing novels was not my dad's thing.

My dad was an automobile junkie. That was his thing. He loved to work on and race cars. But he didn't tease me or try to prevent me from tapping into my true nature. Because of that, I have gotten to spend years filled with the joy that's come from reading and writing books.

So, while you may have ideas about what you'd like to see your child doing as an adult, don't push and don't repress or try to extinguish your child's true nature. Instead, celebrate your child's artistic, social, career, academic, financial, spiritual, athletic, and other authentic aims.

After all, the constant push to excel or please others, including a parent, causes a child pain. More specifically, *Greater Good Magazine* says, "Cultural messages that kids absorb about having to be great at everything and look good doing it compound the pressure to perform. When children inevitably fall short of perfection, they may feel crushed by shame and either give up or push themselves so hard that they find no joy in their lives."[7]

To avoid steering your child away from his true nature, focus on building your child's confidence. That way, he'll tap into the strength to follow inner guidance and trust in the outcome of that guidance. According to *Psychology Today*, here are a few ways you could build your child's confidence as well as nurture the development of his true nature:

- Observe and learn your child's personality and areas where there is opportunity for growth or improvement.
- "When your child is not 'living up to their potential,' is hypersensitive or anxious, and/or is avoidant, be sure not to communicate negative belittling messages that convey your disapproval, frustration, or disappointment in who they are. Avoid statements like "you are a baby," "what is wrong with you?" or "you're lazy."[8]
- Be aware of subliminal messages you give and receive from your child. "If you are always cautioning them to take risks — you may also be communicating that they are unable to handle things, cannot make decisions on their own, and are generally not capable or trustworthy to do so."
- Aim to build internal fulfillment instead of external approval in your child.
- Present your child with achievable and age-appropriate tasks.

- Make it clear that no one can make us feel any emotion. Our perceptions are the cause of what we feel. Furthermore, "Your children can learn to build confidence by identifying what insecurity is surfacing, why and how it is being highlighted for them, and what part of them they can look to work on and improve."[8]

As your child's confidence strengthens and you continue to give your child the freedom to be who they truly are -- who knows? Your child could become a talented painter, writer, musician, educator, athlete, minister, scientist, archeologist, social worker, community leader, farmer, mountain climber, etc. If you push them to try to become a successful chief executive officer, entrepreneur, actress, lawyer, physician, etc. and your child gives in to your demands, your child might become a success in the career. What your child probably won't do is feel authentic and genuinely happy.

Furthermore, not only will your child gain as you allow their true nature to come through. You'll gain. As a mom, you'll get to watch your child blossom into greatness (being their true self is real greatness) right in front of your eyes.

Start Early

BBC shares that infants can hear while in the womb. Dr. Danielle Matthews says, "From the third trimester of pregnancy, babies start hearing speech. They're not picking up on individual words or sounds. Instead, everything sounds muffled to them: they're surrounded by liquid in the womb so what they can hear sounds like what we hear when we're underwater."[9]

She continues, "But they are able to pick up on the prosody of language. This is the rhythm and melody of your voice and it's a really important part of language development."

Hence, it might not be too early to start reading or singing to your child. Don't wait until your child turns 7 or 12 years old to start parenting. That's too late.

Concerning starting early, in addition to what you say, your mood and energy also impact your child. Even if you're dealing with a stressful situation like a job layoff, breakup, or a tough school project, commit to relax. Why? Energy may transfer from person to person.

Bioenergetics is a scientific field that studies energy's transformation in cells and living organisms. About the science of bioenergetics Lifehack shares, "The universe and everything in it is comprised of atoms, which are in part made up of energy." Additionally, "The human body is very similar to a plant that sucks and absorbs the energy needed to feed your emotional state."[10]

In everyday situations, you'll be presented with countless opportunities to check your mood or energy. For example, if you're seeking employment, instead of looking for a job three to four hours a day, building tension inside your internal system, you could search and apply for jobs for a maximum of one hour a day four days a week. Then, pray and trust that the right job will be yours.

It also helps to start early to guide your child toward a rewarding adulthood. If your child enjoys a long physical journey, they will spend a lot more years as an adult than as a child. Toward this end, you could identify resources to help your child develop into a healthy adult. Examples of these resources include:

- Mentoring organizations (e.g., Girls, Inc., Big Brothers/Big Sisters, 4-H)
- Understood (an organization that links parents and children to licensed professionals)
- Find a Mentor (they list several mentoring organizations)

- National Dissemination Center for Children with Disabilities
- Council for Exceptional Children
- Tribal organizations that support women and mothers
- National Youth Leadership
- Local Arts Programs (you could find these at schools, libraries, or private organizations)
- Volunteer Organizations (e.g., Best Friends, Safe Haven)
- Tutoring (e.g., Kumon Learning Center, Tutors for Kids)

Also consider bringing your child to work with you. The goal isn't for your child to do labor but to start becoming familiar with the work environment. After your child enters second or third grade, you could sign them up to participate in a Take Our Kids to Work Day event at your job.

Overall, focus on your child's natural path. As a tip, consider searching online and in local offline directories for organizations and digital tools you can use to support your child early.

Be Consistent

Although starting early is good, it's not enough. To be effective, you must reinforce what you teach your child. School teachers and coaches repeat lessons for this very reason. The University of Nebraska-Lincoln shares, "During stressful times, consistency heightens performance and well-being."[11]

If you tell your child not to kick, bite, or throw objects, sit your child down each time you catch them doing this. Repeat the lesson in a way that's intended to guide, not to do harm.

Parenting really is a life skill. Watch the results of your efforts. Stay free of using verbal, emotional, or physical abuse with your child. It doesn't matter how frustrated you feel, parent with love.

Consistency also means that you don't discipline your child based on how you feel. Sit your child down right away if they kick, bite, or throw objects even if you're not feeling agitated. It might help to see yourself as your child's primary life teacher.

Create routines that offer consistency. Examples of this include waking your child around the same time and eating breakfast, lunch, and dinner around the same time.

Soon your child will become accustomed to the routines. But also allow room for spontaneity. While being consistent, familiarize yourself with milestones[12] that children generally experience as well as tips to help kids develop healthy habits[13]. Milestones might help you spot areas where your child needs additional support. The awareness might also help you identify areas where you need to tweak parenting strategies, becoming consistent in different ways.

Although this list is not conclusive, it highlights typical age milestones children display. For a more complete list and fuller details on the milestones, please see the reference section at the back of this book.

- **13 months old** – Children start to experience separation anxiety. They might cry and worry when they don't see a primary caretaker nearby. Children also require about 9 hours of sleep during this stage and may start throwing fierce tantrums.
- **Two years** – Your child's personality starts to blossom.
- **Three years** – Imagination rules! Some children might have imaginary friends or create robust dreams. Play is another area where imagination is on display.
- **Four years** – Although still a toddler, your child is developing more, including expanding their vocabulary.
- **Five years** - This is a time when your child starts to become more independent and confident.

"Being someone's mom is a personal journey, beautifully shared between mother and child."

Chapter 4 – A Personal Journey

Each single mom has her own parenting journey. This is yours. Sure. You can share experiences, ups and downs, triumphs and lessons learned with other single moms. But only you can walk out your journey.

There will be parenting strategies that work well for you but that are ineffective for other single moms and vice versa. Listen to your Higher Self. Seek the Creator's guidance as you look for ways to:

- Deepen or clear your communications with your child
- Teach your child to forgive
- Demonstrate to your child that it's safe to take smart risks
- Balance having fun with your child with leading and guiding your child
- Educate your child about finances (in age-appropriate and non fear-based ways), especially during times when your child requests more material things, showing that they are starting to link happiness with money and buying
- Sharpen your child's academic focus
- Help your child deal with peer pressure
- Adjust as your child grows up, changing your focus

Deep within, you know what to do. If you're unable to hear inner guidance, you might find well researched books helpful. Definitely get still. A still mind can hear the Creator.

Also, keep the ultimate goal in mind. For example, you're not trying to raise a child who spells well, runs fast, or knows the answers to complicated math equations.

The ultimate goal is to raise a loving, joy-filled, well-balanced adult, someone who has the confidence and the know-how to work with the Creator to design a life they love. As a single mom, it wouldn't be a stretch to think that you also have a goal to live a beautiful life of your own, while you're parenting and after your child grows up.

Begin now to make decisions that allow both goals to be fulfilled.

No Better Mom

If you want to be happy, avoid comparing your parenting skills with other single moms'. And avoid comparing your child's development with any other child's.

Signs that you're comparing yourself or your child to another single mom or to another child vary. Here are some general signs that you can look for:

- Encouraging your child to read, spell, count or recite the alphabet in front of another child or another parent
- Feeling a sting of embarrassment, shame or anger should you witness another child outperforming your child in a sport, academics, arts, in a volunteer effort, etc.
- Bragging excessively to another mom about how well your child is doing
- Pushing your child to study more, excel soon after you hear about a child who won an award or who was featured on television or another type of media (e.g., magazine, newspaper, website)

Additionally, if you push yourself too hard, potentially slipping into burnout, it could be a sign that you've compared yourself to another parent and "don't want to fall behind" – in turn, becoming eager to do something that shows you're an equally good (or better) parent. Instead of engaging in comparisons, do the best that you can.

This means that you do the best you can with what you know *now*. Years after giving birth, you'll know more than you did when your child was born.

Don't rush the learning process. You will get there. Trust your true Self.

An Uninterrupted Path

Have you ever been driven to do something you didn't want to do? Perhaps you were driven to work long hours, stay in a dead-end relationship or live in a home that doesn't work for you energetically.

Take a moment to think about those experiences. Reflect on times when you felt "forced" to do something. It doesn't matter who was pushing you to take a path that's not right for you. For one reason or another, you allowed yourself to be pushed / forced down a path that you realize was wrong for you.

You might find it helpful to get a pen and pad and write down your reflections. Or you could write your reflections in the space below. In addition to writing about the specific act you felt forced to do that you now know wasn't right for you, write about emotions and thoughts you experienced while you were on this "wrong for you" path.

_____

_____

_____

_____

_____

_____

_____

_____

_____

_____

Next, reflect on times when you absolutely knew that you were doing something that is right for you, something that makes you thrive, feel empowered and energized. Write about these activities. Also, write about how you feel and think as you engage in the activities.

_____

_____

_____

_____

_____

_____

_____

_____

_____

_____

Being a single mom doesn't mean that you must forfeit your passions or your dreams. You can do both (parent and pursue your dreams), especially if you do what you love, are on the right path and don't compare yourself to others.

The longer you parent, the more you might notice how the life lessons you learn benefit your child. For instance, the more you see how following the wrong path, life choices that have been forced upon you, de-energizes you, the less you may be tempted to try to force your child onto a path that's wrong for them.

Witness

Remember how you recorded your child's weight and height at birth, marveling at the miracle before you? Your eager, attentive gaze caught each of your child's smiles, yawns, squirms, and wiggles.

For months, you may have written down your precious baby's weight and a series of first: when your baby first rolled over, held up her head, slept longer than three hours at night, etc. Over the coming years, you might ask your child to stand against a wall, tape measure in hand, so you can track their growth.

There is a wealth of rewarding experiences to witness as a parent. Count yourself as fortunate if you witness dozens of the many "firsts" in your child's life.

Several events you witness will happen seemingly out-of-the-blue. You might scream with excitement as you watch your child:

- Hold their head up
- Crawl for the first time
- Take those celebrated first steps
- Smile at you and say, "Mama"
- Put their toys away independently, without so much as a word of instruction from you
- Sleep soundly through the night
- Eat all their vegetables absent fuss
- Graduate from kindergarten
- Ride a bicycle without training wheels

- Catch the school bus on their own
- Dress themselves
- Prepare their own breakfast
- Walk the dog or clean up after the cat
- Read their favorite book to you
- Make their bed before heading outside to play

Catch as many "firsts" as you can. Use your smartphone to record videos and pictures of your child's firsts. Also capture your child's carefree voice on audiotapes and videos. Back pictures and videos up on flash drives. Even journal about your child's firsts and continuing development.

It's these videos, audiotapes, pictures, and journals that your child may love revisiting after they are an adult. You really are in a blessed position as a single mom. Don't wait until your child is grown and gone from home before you realize this.

"Trust is a key ingredient in a lovely life."

Chapter 5 – Trust the Process

It's true! Children aren't born with a roadmap or an instruction manual that you can refer to. Instead, you must trust the process.

Not trusting the process comes at a high price, especially if you don't have family and friends nearby, people you can bounce concerns and ideas off. Try to figure everything out yourself, and you could lose sleep (not to mention peace) over a myriad of situations you and/or your child experience, including:

- Extreme emotional shifts
- Child crying frequently during the day and/or night
- Symptoms from *unknown* allergies
- Brain functions that cause your child to need special care
- Money woes that prevent you from getting your child toys or clothes they want, that make it hard to pay basic bills
- Growing demands at work that leave you facing deepening fatigue, all while you must access the energy to parent effectively
- Your child's father being aggressive, abusive, controlling or absent, despite your efforts to co-parent in a healthy way

Situations you might face could extend beyond the above-mentioned. However, by themselves, the above situations could rob you of sleep – if you let them. Even if you do sleep, you might never sleep deeply for more than one to two hours a night. That lack of sleep could push you into impatience and irritation.

Plainly put, you need sound sleep. Your mind needs to rest. Peace should be a part of your life. The only way to let yourself be empowered with peace is to trust the process. Looking for ways to build trust? Try these:

- Pray and let go of what you prayed for (don't worry how it will unfold)
- Meditate on scriptures and other writings that spotlight the benefits of trusting the Creator
- Keep a journal, tracking the outcome of prayers, meditations, and results you work for. List dates when you receive what you requested. The more you see your requests being fulfilled, the easier it may become to trust.
- Read biographies and autobiographies of people who trusted in good outcomes against seemingly insurmountable odds. Pay attention to how these people's trust paid off in amazingly good ways.

Parenting is a long journey. As much as you might want to, you can't see all that is coming. It might not sound sexy, but you really do only have two choices. You can worry and make yourself sick, weakening your parenting skills, or you can trust the process.

Force Free Living

Believe it or not, you're growing with your child. There's a harvest of experiences ahead for both of you. Yes. You're a single mom, but your child is not the only one in the relationship who's seeing things through a new lens.

Because you're a loving parent, you know that you must be patient with your child whether your child is learning to write, read, play a new game, or navigate the world of social skills and friendships. What you might not have told yourself is that *you also must be patient with yourself*.

If this is your first-time parenting, this bears repeating -- you have never raised a child before. You may make mistakes. Forgive yourself.

You will achieve huge successes both your child and you will benefit greatly from. Celebrate those good achievements. Keep going. There should be more successes ahead.

Don't force things. Don't force yourself to *suddenly* become as effective a parent as your mom, grandmother, older sister, aunt, or an older friend are. They have parented a child to adulthood. You haven't.

They know about the push and pull, the ups and downs and back and forth inherent in parenting. You're still learning about those shifts.

Not forcing outcomes aligns with not comparing your parenting efforts (or your child's development) to anyone else's, even your best friend. Here's one surprising area where not forcing pays off – potty training.

I remember when my son was about 18 months old. I wanted him to be potty trained before he turned two. Before I knew it, I was feeling disappointed, like a failure and angry when my son pooped on himself (better to pee than poop, I thought for some strange reason).

Inner wisdom shared a question – "Have you seen a healthy 40-year-old wearing a diaper because they poop and pee on their self?"

After lingering in thought for a moment, I realized that I hadn't. That fact gifted me with the assurance that my son would, indeed, get potty trained. Fortunately, my son's babysitter told me that *forcing* the potty training would make the training harder for my son and me.

"When your son is ready to be potty trained, it will be so easy. He'll start going to the potty or telling you that he needs to go to the bathroom on his own. When he's ready, it shouldn't take more than a few days."

I could hardly believe what my son's babysitter was saying. But turns out, she was right. Within a few weeks, my son started showing signs that he was ready to be potty trained. Once he was ready, it only took three days for him to start going to the bathroom on his own.

To this day, that potty training lesson remains one of the more impactful lessons that I've had. You might see the benefits of not forcing things at home, at work and in other areas of your social and personal life.

Regardless of the specific challenge, these steps could help you to let go, no longer demanding to control outcomes. These steps could also help you to trust the process and let go of fear and worry. See which ones work for you:

- Decide where you want to be or what you want to accomplish.
- Access where you are now.
- Identify actions you could take to close the gap between where you are now and where you want to be.
- Get clear about what you can control and what you can't. Let go of what you can't control, trusting the Creator to ensure all works out well.
- Focus on what could go right instead of what could go wrong.
- If you're still tempted to worry, get a watch, and allow yourself to worry for two minutes, then stop. Shift your thoughts to something love-based.
- Make a list of what you learn from mistakes. Take these lessons with you like priceless gifts.
- Keep trying.
- Celebrate your progress, regardless of how big or small.
- Count your blessings.
- Pursue "progress" instead of "perfection".

About School

School is an area that can either lift you up, filling you with hope and promise, or push you into ongoing stress. For instance, if you're not certain about your parenting skills or how amazing your child innately is, just one bad report from school could send you into stress. Soon you could start mentally accusing your child's teacher of being ineffective, not liking your child, zoning in on your child or lacking quality teaching skills.

School is also an area that can build or strip away your child's confidence. If you link your child's school performance to their worth, how smart they really are, their level of discipline and how good their future can be, school report cards can feel like rewards or weapons.

The way you respond to grades your child gets on their report card can have a deep and lasting impact. Let's say your child brings home a "C", "D" or Heaven forbid, the most dreaded "F" on their report card. A look of disappointment, anger, or fear from you could send a message to your child that what they do isn't good enough. Let this scene repeat each time your child brings a report card home, and your child might grow anxious days before the end of a grading period. That or your child might consider running away just to avoid facing you while you look over their grades. (I made good grades in school, but once I got a "D" in a class and considered running away to avoid facing my dad.) Or your child might alter grades on the report card or be tempted to forge your signature, all to avoid having to face your reactions to their grades.

And again, if your child links your reactions to their grades to how you genuinely feel and think about them, the result could be damaging. Early signs that damage may have occurred could show up in your child as:

- Body aches (e.g., headaches, stomach aches) before it's time to head to school
- Trouble sleeping
- Worry or anxiety
- Poor confidence
- Constant concern about what you think of them
- Lack of focus in and out of school
- Worsening school performance
- Diminished communication with you
- Attempts to show off in effort to prove to you how good they are (this could come thru overexerting themselves in sports, dangerous risk taking or other daring endeavors)

Sit down and talk with your child as soon as you spot one of the above signs or another sign that your child is suffering due to the link between school performance and how they think you perceive them. Make sure that your child knows that you value them, regardless of how they perform in school.

Certainly, encourage your child to do their best in school and elsewhere and get your child tutoring support if needed, but don't link performance to worth.

That means that you don't link your child's worth (in your eyes) to how they perform in school. It also means that you don't link *your worth* as a parent to how your child performs in school, which raises a good point.

Should you become particularly upset with your child due to school grades, you might be upset, in large part, because you fear the grades show the teacher, your parents, other students and their parents, etc. that you're not a good parent. This is a good time to learn an important life lesson.

Nothing in this world determines your worth. Your worth is established by the Creator; your immeasurable worth will never change. There isn't anything in this world that mirrors your worth – your worth is that limitless, that amazing, that wonderful – that indescribable.

Regardless of how you have responded to your child as it relates to school, fortunately, you have a lot of leverage where your child's confidence is concerned. As a start, to strengthen your child's confidence, steer clear of linking your child's worth to the way your child performs at anything.

Other actions you can take to strengthen your child's confidence include:

- Play with your child. Set aside time each day to do nothing except have fun with your child.
- Read to your child.
- Let your child read to you absent you repeatedly correcting how they speak, sit, etc.
- Allow your child to prepare part of the morning or evening meal. Don't change what your child prepares. Simply enjoy it.

- Give your child the right to pick out their own clothes and wear those clothes.
- Listen to your child when she is speaking with you. Put your cell phone, tablet, and other distractions away. If you find it helpful, remind yourself that your child will be an adult sooner than you think. The time to listen to your child while she's still young will soon be gone, so do it now.
- Ask your child about their school day, what they're learning and how they feel about school. Also ask your child if there's anything they want to talk to you about.
- Let your child feed and care for a family pet.
- Celebrate your child's creative endeavors.
- Share stories of how you struggled in school (don't make stories up) or in another educational or social environment with your child.
- Talk with your child about their interests, activities you notice them being attracted to (e.g., music, painting, writing, teaching, science, technology). Show them how education and postsecondary certifications and degrees could aid them in careers that align with their passions.

Also, instead of making school grades a priority, make your child's overall inner and outer well-being top priority. Approaching school month-by-month or academic-period-by-academic-period could also help. It's less weighty than looking at school as if your child's performance during the first week will remain unchanged throughout the entire school year.

Keeping in touch with your child's teacher could also prove beneficial. The goal isn't to become the teacher's friend.

The goal is to make the teacher comfortable with reaching out to you should they see a shift in your child. A sign that this might be working is when your child's teacher emails you to tell you how well your child is doing in school.

After all, no healthy relationship only involves communication when something is amiss. Within the umbrella of a healthy relationship, communication shares impressively good news.

Put Yourself on Time Out

When the world was coming out of the COVID19 shutdown, work picked up significantly for me. Based on my childhood programming, I knew I was going to do what it took to keep up with the increasing work volume.

My elders taught my siblings and me to work hard and that working hard yielded good results. For example, my elders taught us that if we worked hard and put our all into work that we did, we'd always have a job. When I got laid off during the Great Recession, I knew what they'd told me wasn't true.

That didn't stop my programming from going into effect as work shifted as we came out of COVID19 shutdown. Because of my programming, I did whatever it took to keep up. What I didn't know was that the volume of work would continue to increase.

Thankfully, I did let organizational leaders know that I couldn't keep taking on more and more. Another thing that I did was to pull back on volunteer work.

It was helpful, but not enough. Colleagues let me know that it was good to step back, rest and recharge.

Finally, that's what I did. And did I ever feel better after taking more than a week away from work. Looking back, that's probably the fourth or fifth time something like that has happened to me. Oddly, I didn't know how much stress I was carrying until I took a break.

As an example, and before I took the break, on Saturday afternoons, around 2pm or 3pm, I started to notice that I felt happy, recharged, and energetically open. That's when I knew something was wrong. It was taking until late Saturday afternoon for me to feel stress free.

During the week, I hadn't noticed how much stress I was carrying. Fortunately, I practice awareness, so the message that I was carrying too much stress did come through on those Saturdays.

That's just one example of what going-going-going and taking on more-more-more could do. Your work as a single mom might extend beyond raising a child.

In addition to being a single mom, you might work a demanding job remotely or outside your home. Additionally, you might help care for an aging parent or grandparent and volunteer in the community.

Even if your main role is to care for your child, that's a significant undertaking. Practice awareness. Pay attention to how you feel. Be aware of your thoughts, spotting when you feel increasing stress, frustrated, disappointed, angry, or sad.

Tap into your support system, asking a friend or relative if they're agreeable to watching your child for two to three hours so you can get a break. Don't become upset if they say "no" and don't try to force them, perhaps enticing them with guilt, to watch your child.

In fact, it's good to have options. For example, you could:

- Build and expand a trustworthy support system
- Help care for a friend's child to give the friend a break and vice versa
- Join a loving single mom support group, the type of group that goes on weekend trips, visits museums, etc. together. Through the support group, you could gain assistance with looking after your child while your child has fun at a museum, park, beach, etc. with other kids their age.
- Create a schedule for when your child will spend time with their father
- Take your child on nature trips, places where you automatically de-stress. Enjoy this time with your child.

Other ways to regularly rest are to let your child play with neighborhood friends and to enroll your child in a local camp. Do your homework and *ensure everyone* at the camp is safe and healthy to be around, allowing your child to be in the care of responsible, trustworthy, and harmless adults.

When my son was in middle school, one of his friend's moms asked me if I'd watch her son while she made an international call to her mother. I said, "Sure."

That's one way single moms get a break. To repeat, ensure that you ask someone if they're agreeable to watching your child. Don't just drop your child off at someone's house.

To rest and recharge, retire to bed early enough to enter deep sleep. Turning off the television and putting away your cell phone, tablet, etc. could improve your sleep, again allowing you to enter deep sleep and fully recharge.

Set a bedtime schedule for your children that allows you to enjoy one or more hours of relaxation alone before you head to bed. That or you could awaken one to two hours before your children get out of bed, again giving yourself time to relax in quiet.

Get creative. Find a way to relax and recharge once a day and over the weekend.

Should you feel overwhelmed, consider inviting your older children to play outdoors while you sit down and rest. You could also talk with a relative or friend, gifting yourself with support and care.

As colleagues shared with me, it is your responsibility to ensure you rest, relax and recharge. Make it a daily priority. It's a great way to empower yourself as a single mom. It's a great way to prove that you do love yourself.

"Choosing better relationships is part of growing up."

Chapter 6 – Relationships

Relationships, platonic and intimate, will take center stage in your life, hopefully for as long as you're in this world. Desiring the sweetness of a romantic relationship is natural. You deserve to be treasured, pampered, loved, and adored.

Desire to be in a romantic relationship is so common that, in the United States alone, approximately 35% of Americans have paid a monthly dating app fee. In fact, people pay more than $100 a month on dating apps, some paying $400 a month. As reported at CNBC, men as well as adults between 50-64 years old are among the highest dating app users.[14]

That doesn't mean that younger adults aren't turning to dating apps and/or dating coaches. They are. The youngest users mentioned in the CNBC article were 18 years old. Why are people turning to dating coaches and dating apps?

There are a variety of reasons, including the belief that it's harder to meet quality dates offline. Adults share that it's hard to juggle work and dating several people you meet in person until you find the "right one" in today's fast-paced world.

So, you're not alone in wanting to share your life with a romantic partner. It's natural. Meet the right partner, someone who's fully ready mentally, spiritually, financially, and emotionally to enter and sustain a healthy, loving relationship, and you could enjoy years of love, joy, and peace.

Even more, you're an amazing woman. But it's not always easy to carve out time to date and nurture a romantic relationship as a single mom. If your ex is vindictive or has a difficult time letting go of the relationship the two of you once had, dating again could hit bumps in the road.

Attempts by your ex to keep you from getting completely free might look like:

- Last minute notices that a meeting, emergency, etc. suddenly came up, causing him to be unable to keep your child, hopefully preventing you from being able to go on a date
- Unannounced visits to your home, moments before the man you're currently dating is set to arrive
- So called "emergency" cell phone calls with your ex rambling while, across the table from you at a restaurant, the new guy you're dating sits and waits for you to get off the phone

As if that's not enough, your ex might coach your child to make life difficult for the new man you're dating. This could come in the form of tantrums, incessant whimpering, pouting, stoic looks or arguments.

If you want to date again without fighting with your ex or dealing with unnecessary upset from your child, get out in front of the dating routine – fun, challenges, surprises, and all! To do this, set aside quiet time to talk with your child.

Of course, if your child is too young, you could skip this step. For instance, if your child never met their biological father or if your child is seven years or younger, talking with your child about dating could be confusing for your child. For older children, it helps if you're open to answering their questions about why you and their father are no longer together.

Should your child be old enough to question why you are no longer in a relationship with their father, simply and gently tell your child that you and their father will always be in their life, but that you are no longer dating or married. Set aside time to answer your child's questions. Don't rush the conversation.

It could take days, weeks or months before your child fully understands that the relationship between their father and you has changed. In fact, your child might try to do or say things that they think could cause you and their father to get back together.

Relate shares that it's helpful to listen to your child without taking sides and give your child time to accept the change. Additionally, "Consider that the fact you're getting divorced from their father/mother may be a huge shock to them even though you've been thinking about it/been aware this could happen for some time."[15]

Furthermore, "Remember that, very often, whatever you're feeling, they very much love and want to spend time with you and their father. They may feel very torn and disloyal at not living with you both."

To repeat, don't try to force your child to see the situation your way. If you've recently separated from your child's father or are going through a divorce, you may find it beneficial to review the *Forbes* "Divorce Checklist: 15 Dos and Don'ts In 2023".[16] (see References) Specifically, "Try to avoid blaming your spouse, badmouthing your spouse in front of the kids or forcing your kids to choose between you during the divorce process. This can make life harder for your children, and it could backfire because the court could decide you're engaging in parental alienation and opt to give primary custody to the other parent because of this misbehavior."[16]

After your child starts to accept that their parents' relationship has ended, it may be time to speak with your child about dating again, if that's what you've decided to do. To begin, introduce your child to someone you're serious about. Avoid introducing your child to casual dates, as this could confuse your child and put their safety at risk, especially if you don't know the person well yourself.

Go slowly. Your child didn't choose to have this person in their life. Who you're dating might not feel close to your child either. Spend time dining, visiting a park, etc. as a trio before telling your child that you want to enter a long-term relationship with the person.

Consider asking your child how they feel about you dating again. Should your child be especially against you dating, ask them why. According to Newsweek, "Staying compassionate with one's self and with each other's real thoughts and feelings rather than reaching for the ideal family scene can make all the difference."[17]

If your ex has proven to be difficult or emotionally, mentally, or physically abusive, it could prove beneficial to let the man you're dating know about your ex, keeping in mind that the point is to *ensure everyone is safe*.

Throughout the dating process, be open to speaking with your child about how they are handling you dating. Do this especially if you notice your child struggling.

Signs that your child is struggling could manifest in the form of withdrawing, constantly rejecting or turning away from you, sadness, or impulsivity. Be there for your child even as your romantic life changes.

More ways to create a healthy dating environment deal with respect, time management and open mindedness. Among these actions, you could:

- Set clear guidelines around the days/times when you will be on a date
- Reinforce the importance of respecting self and others to your child
- Encourage your child to let you know if someone you're dating, your ex, etc. causes them to feel afraid or coerced into doing something they don't want to do (set clear rules around "touch" and psychological and verbal abuse)
- Keep promises. This means that you depart and return from dates when you say you will.

What you say and do should send a clear message to your child that they are top priority. If your child senses that you've put them on the back burner while placing the new man in your life before them, it could cause your child to doubt their place of importance in your life.

Engaging in the right conversations with your child and your ex (if it's safe to communicate with your ex) in smart ways could take a lot of stress out of dating someone new. Taking the right actions, including keeping promises that you make, could give your child the confidence and comfort of knowing that you'll always be there for them, loving them as deeply as you did before you started dating again.

This is a new and exciting time in your life. Who knows? You could be dating someone you'll enjoy years of romantic love and care with. Your child might even come to love who you're dating. Just don't force your child to like your beau. Instead, allow the relationship to develop naturally and safely.

And let yourself be loved and cared for. Have fun. Relax while a member of your support system looks after your child during times when you're at a restaurant, movie, etc. with the new person in your life.

You deserve to be loved. You deserve to be cherished. While you're receiving this from someone else, make sure that you also do it for yourself. Simply put – love yourself regardless of your relationship status.

Leaving Bad Relationships in the Past

It's amazing how hard it can be to let a bad relationship go. One kind conversation, a gentle hug and before you know it, you're recalling the early parts of the relationship, good times you shared with your child's father.

You know you've been here before, maybe dozens of times. Each time it starts and ends the same, wit-h you feeling poorly, neglected, and unloved.

This time, get off the merry-go-round. Stop going in circles that go nowhere good.

Let the bad relationship go. Just let it go.

Hang on to bad relationships and you could teach your child to live a "stuck life". You could teach your child that it's more important to be in a romantic relationship (even if that relationship is abusive) than it is to be safe, healthy and on your own.

Even if you don't want them to, your child is watching you. In fact, your child could be watching you more closely than anyone else ever will.

The way you manage yourself in relationships, including bad relationships, could signal to your child that it's the best way to manage all relationships. Allow yourself to be disrespected, talked down to and manipulated and your child might convince themselves that it's okay to accept mistreatment.

Scream and shout at your partner when you're trying to get a point across, and your child might learn that talking at the top of their lungs is the best way to ensure they're heard. Strike your partner or allow yourself to be struck and you could (as much as you might not want to) teach your child that this behavior is okay in romantic relationships.

Not wanting something to happen doesn't stop it from happening. If you want your child to know what a loving relationship looks and feels like, you need to leave bad relationships that you're in – safely -- and start to love yourself.

Introducing Your Child to New People

We are incredibly impressionable as children. Add to that the fact that, because the world is new during childhood, it's easy for a child to believe what they hear or what they see.

If your child is a toddler or in elementary school, they might think the man you're dating is honest, trustworthy, and caring *simply because you're with him*. Think about this before you introduce your child to someone.

This includes someone you're dating, a colleague, girlfriend, someone from the worship center you attend, who you met at a social event, a neighbor or someone you met online. Make sure that you really know the person you want to introduce your child to.

In other words, don't introduce your child to someone you've just met. You should feel comfortable with the person and know enough about them to describe them in a 5,000-word biography.

Yes. You should truly know the person.

Also, set boundaries as it regards the people in your child's life. Oddly enough, if you and your child's father are at odds and have an abrasive relationship, it wouldn't be shocking if you set harder boundaries for him than you do for a total stranger.

"Bring our daughter back by seven o'clock tonight. Don't be late." "I don't want you roughing it with our son. I don't want him fighting or hanging out with your tough-as-nails friends. And make sure you put a coat on our son before he goes out in the rain or snow." "Make sure you are the one watching the kids. Don't drop them off at your parents, expecting them to babysit. It's your weekend to parent the kids, spend time with them this weekend." "I don't want your girlfriend telling our kids what to do or disciplining them. Make sure you're with our kids the entire time your girlfriend is at your place."

That might be a short list of to-dos as it regards the reminders and instructions you leave with your child's father moments before he pulls out of the driveway with your child in the front or back seat. Have you ever asked yourself why you aren't as particular with other people your child is around?

You don't pause for five minutes to consider how many demands, instructions, and warnings (you might even throw in a few threats) you give your child's father when he comes to pick your child up for several hours or for the weekend. If you did the same with other people, word might get around that you don't play games when it comes to setting people straight as it regards your child's care.

Everyone in your neighborhood, at the organization where you work, in your family, at school and beyond would know not to mess with your child.

Why are you so tough on your child's father, if you are? It's likely because you've seen the best side and the side with room for the most improvement in your child's father. You've seen the side of your child's father that you thought so much of, that caused you to desire to share the remainder of your life with him. Time passing, you later were a witness to parts of your child's father (e.g., criticalness, grudge holding, anger) that is a turnoff.

Ask questions if you must. Get to know people who know the people you want to bring into your child's life. Yes. Really get to know the people you want to introduce to your child.

Make it a priority to get to know them well, their good and not so great personality traits and habits, *before* you add them to your child's life. Accept facts you uncover about this person. Don't create blind spots or act like you don't know what you do just so you can feel "okay" about being with the person. It's a great way to keep your child safe, which is covered more thoroughly in the next chapter.

Keeping Your Child Safe

As shared in the previous chapter, ensuring that you know the people you introduce your child to *before* you bring these people into your child's life, is one of the best ways to keep your child safe. So too is being with your child and the people your child interacts with.

Do this without becoming controlling. To keep your child safe, also set clear boundaries for your child and each person your child is with, especially people your child is alone with. Only leave your child alone with people you know extremely well. Boundaries you could set include:

- No fighting with or around your child
- Bullying and verbal threats are not permitted
- No sexual texts, touching, movies or conversation
- Limit television watching to an hour a day (or whatever limit you prefer)
- Keep technology like smartphone and video game usage to an hour a day
- Use caring and responsible language

It's also important to talk with your child about healthy boundaries. In fact, a lot (if not all) of the boundaries that you set for other children and adults who are with your child may be boundaries that you set for your child when they're with you. For instance, at home you might limit the time your child spends watching television, playing video games, and engaging with friends on a tablet or computer.

Your child would be accustomed to these boundaries. But that doesn't mean your child won't try to break those boundaries when they're away from you. In fact, that's exactly what your child might try to do.

So, speak with your child about healthy boundaries. Also, let your child know why you have set boundaries. For example, you might tell your child that you're limiting their television time because you want your child to enjoy playing outdoors with their friends.

Even more, you could go on to share with your child how you wished you had spent more time playing outdoors with friends when you were your child's age. That or you could share with your child how much fun you had playing at the park, in the back yard or on your friend's front porch as a kid.

Tell your child about the healthy boundaries and rules your parents set that you adhered to. Let your child know how those rules benefited you. Doing so could strengthen your child and your relationship and communication. I remember my dad telling us how his parents advised him and his two sisters to be home before the streetlight came on. My siblings and I laughed at this, especially considering that our dad also told us to be home before the streetlight came on.

The better the communication between your child and you, the more you two can partner to keep your child safe. After all, it's good communication that allows your child to feel comfortable enough to tell you anything. This includes things that bother, scare, or worry your child.

Tell your child not to let anyone stroke their hair, hands, or other body parts, or kiss them on the mouth. But don't stop there.

Ask your child to tell you if anyone speaks to or looks at them in a way that makes them feel uncomfortable, as if someone is trying to manipulate or control them, including if your child feels as if the person is flirting with them. Share grooming signs with your child, not to build distrust for others in your child, but to make your child aware and to keep your child safe.

Safety boundaries you could set with your child include:

- Sharing grooming signs
- Giving examples of age-appropriate conversation
- Telling your child where their "private parts" are and making it crystal clear that no one should touch their genitalia, not to wipe them after they go to the toilet or to straighten their clothes – for no reason.
- Making it clear to your child that they should immediately tell you and the nearest adult (if you're not

around when the event occurs) that someone tried to (or did) touch them inappropriately.

Be clear with your child about what a secret is and different types of secrets. Tell your child not to make or keep secrets that put them in danger. If someone threatens your child saying they'll harm them or that you'll be harmed if your child tells you about a wrong the person did, encourage your child to tell you.

Staying safe, without becoming controlling or guided by fear, is the top priority. Fortunately, if you do your homework and get to know people you allow around your child *before* the people start spending time with your child, you can become aware of people who have already exhibited unhealthy desires, conversation, and behavior.

Trust what you feel and what you see and hear when you're around people, especially as it regards your child's safety. It's these same lessons that can benefit your child, now and into adulthood. Here are some online and offline tools, including apps, that aim to keep kids safe (links effective as of January 2024):

- Consumers Advocate: Top 10 Parental Control Apps of 2024 (consumersadvocate.org)
- Cleveland Clinic: Internet Safety for Kids: Online Safety Tips (clevelandclinic.org)
- Psychology Today: Helping Children Stay Safe Online and Offline | Psychology Today
- CDC – Caring for Children in a Disaster: Keeping Children Safe | CDC

Getting Love

No one is going to love you more than you do except your Creator. If you've spent a lifetime loving yourself, awesome! If you're learning to love yourself, awesome! Either way, you're on a blessed path!

As tempted as you might feel to search for another person -- someone you perceive to be a safe harbor, someone capable of creating a life tucked inside a "special" relationship you dream of experiencing, someone who will love you the way you want to be loved – know this -- no one else can love you *for you*. Therefore, get serious about learning to love yourself.

Why? If you don't, you could spend the remainder of your physical experience seeking someone (wrapped in an attractive body perhaps) who will give you the love that only you can.

[**Tip**: If you want to know how good you are at loving yourself, pay attention to how you love others. Love is complete.

If you feel unloved, there's a good chance that you're not fully giving others love.]

****

To love yourself, accept yourself as you are *in truth*. Begin by seeing yourself as a creation of the greatest Source, an eternal being created as an extension of love.

Also, accept that you cannot recreate yourself, not in reality. That means, mistakes, disappointments, nor poor decisions can turn you into anything you were not created to be.

See yourself the way God created you. It's the truth of what you are. Next, count 10 specific things about yourself that you appreciate. For example, you could appreciate the fact that you:

- Are patient, offering others the time they need to express ideas, learn new skills, etc.
- Approach new situations with an open mind
- Allow people to be who they really are instead of forcing people to fit an idea that you hold of them
- Exercise to care for your body
- Read good books and continue to learn
- Steer clear of gossiping
- Keep in touch with family and friends, reaching out to those you love with intention at least once a week
- Practice sound financial management
- Take full responsibility for your life, including what you think, say, feel, and do
- Strive to love all living beings

Focusing on your positive traits can train your mind to search for good. This can be a shortcut to love, much better than looking for things to criticize.

Watch how people treat those they love. Are there any of these practices that you can add to your life, new and better ways that you can treat yourself?

Ask yourself how you want to be treated. How do you wish another person would treat you, strengthening you with love?

Start to add these actions to your life. Perhaps you can add one new loving activity to your life each week. For instance, if you think being fully listened to is a sign that someone cares about you, start meditating or sitting in silence for 10 minutes a day so you can hear from your true Self.

Be intentional about what you do.

Also, continue to get to know yourself. This could come in the form of journaling, songwriting, dancing, and painting. Another way to get to know yourself is to study the brain, including how the brain functions.

Paying attention to your dreams is another way to learn about yourself. Dreams reveal what's happening at your mind's subconscious level.

These actions bring rewards, including the fact that loving yourself gives you access to increased energy to love your child more deeply. It also helps you realize what real love looks like.

Realizing what real love looks and feels like may protect you from falling for the charms of a man who isn't ready to love, who could end up hurting you. There's so much to gain from loving yourself!

"Money is waiting for you to tell it what to do."

Chapter 7 – Managing Money

Not only does money perception cause relationship splits, but money is also a key reason why many people, including single moms, feel stressed. Depending on where you are in your life, becoming a single mom could put you in a position to learn how to manage money.

Learning this lesson could save you heartache. As happens with learning to love yourself, to begin, find out where you are *now*. Face facts. Stay free of illusions. Forget lying to yourself. Look at your finances and accept what you see.

However, know that just because your finances might be in bad shape *now,* that doesn't mean your money situation will always be bad. But first you must know where you are. To become aware of your financial situation, look at your current money intake and outtake.

Get a spreadsheet or a piece of paper and list how much money, after taxes, you bring in each week. You can also do this across an entire month.

While you record your income, indicate the source for each income item. For example, record how much money you receive from a part-time job, an online remote gig and from selling crafts or artwork that you create. Doing this can help you spot areas where you could increase your income. More about that further into this chapter.

In addition to recording how much money you bring in and the income source, write down how frequently you are paid. Believe it or not, with these simple steps, you're starting to manage your money. Keep reading to learn about debt, reducing debt, building savings, and working with budget templates.[18]

Reducing Debt

Now that you've identified your income sources and how much money you bring in each week (or month), it's time to look at your debt. Similar to how you recorded your income, record how much money you spend each week.

Please don't be like I was the first time I recorded my debt. As much as I wanted to get it right, a part of me didn't want to admit how much money I was spending. This denial rose within me even though I really wasn't spending a lot of money (I didn't have enough income to overspend a lot; my first full-time job after I had my son paid $14,000 gross annually). The issue was that I didn't want to *admit* that I wasn't managing money well.

But I had to get my finances working for me. Eventually (and thankfully), denial lost out to the desire to become financially empowered. Back then, I didn't have an extra dime a day (no kidding) to pay to drive across the toll bridge between Pennsylvania and New Jersey.

So, I sat down, pulled out my check book and got my monthly bank statements. Item by item, expense by expense, I recorded where I was spending money each day, each week, and each month. Here are some of the things I was spending money on. How many of these are familiar?

- Groceries
- Rent
- Car insurance
- Shoes (for me and my son)

- Clothes (for me and my son)
- Movie tickets
- Toys
- Eating out (my son and I had a favorite pizza spot)
- Gas for my car
- Utilities
- Telephone bill
- Books (I love to read!)
- Magazines (I ended up cutting back on magazines)
- Home decorations (I only let myself shop at dollar stores)

I also cut back on shoes, home decorations and, eventually clothes. It started with me recording each item I spent money on, how much I spent on those items and how frequently I made the purchases.

To start reducing your debt, spend an hour (or as long as it takes) recording your expenses in detail. You could spend an hour recording your expenses today and another hour tomorrow or over the weekend. Just ensure you record all expenses. No hiding any spending from yourself.

When you finish, the document you use to record your income and expenses, might look like this:

Net Income

- Part-time job at retail store: $600 a week
- Online freelance writing job: $900 a week
    - Total = $1,500 a week income ($6,000 a month)

Expenses

- Groceries: $65 a week
- Rent: $400 a week
- Utilities: $20 a week
- Car Note: $60 a week
- Car Insurance: $40 a week
- Life Insurance: $30 a week
- Health Insurance: $40 a week
- Eating out: $50 a week
- Clothes: $250 a week
- Shoes: $75 a week
- Toys and video games: $100 a week
- Entertainment (e.g., movies, concerts): $40 a week
- Technology (e.g., cell phone): $30 a week
- Online purchases: $20
-
- 0 a week
- Tithe: $150 a week
- Credit Card: $50 a week
- Car Gas: $40 a week
    - Total = $1,640 weekly expenses

Put your income and expenses on paper and you can see where you're spending your money. You can also see areas where you can start reducing debt.

Look over your income and expenses. To reduce debt, you could increase your income (without increasing your expenses). Or you could only decrease your expenses.

If you pray for a job that pays more, this could be a primary reason why. You know that increasing your income could potentially help reduce your debt.

However, if you don't get clear about your expenses, you could get a raise or a higher paying job only to find yourself in debt within months. Looking back over the example list of expenses, you could reduce clothes, credit card and online purchasing expenses to lower debt.

Yes. It will take discipline, but the payoff is huge. Take it from me, it feels super good (and freeing) when you have savings and extra money on hand every day. And you can.

Be honest with yourself. How much could you reduce your online shopping by? Could you stop making online purchases for six months and see how your savings build?

Could you prepare home-cooked meals and stop eating out for lunch and over the weekends? Instead of catching every movie at the theater, could you stream movies for free at home or go to the movies with a friend or your child once a month?

Also, have you noticed how you feel when you go shopping? Do you feel empowered, excited, hopeful, etc.? Are you using shopping as a drug, shopping to *feel* certain emotions?

If so, consider journaling about how you feel and how you want to feel and how you can bridge the emotional gap in healthy ways, without spending money. Find three or more ways to reduce your expenses, so you spend $200 a week less than your weekly income.

Growing Savings

Reducing your weekly expenses to $200 below your net weekly income is a great start to growing your savings. To sustain these efforts, lose the fear of looking at your bank statements.

In fact, it's good to review your bank statement once or twice a month. As a tip, if you feel afraid to look at your bank statements, you might be overspending and just not want to face it.

It's similar to how you might avoid stepping on the bathroom scale when you know you haven't been eating and exercising in healthy ways. You already know what you're doing. You already know the direction you're headed in. But you don't want to face it.

However, not facing facts doesn't change facts. Not stepping on the bathroom scale won't keep you from gaining weight. Similarly, not looking at your bank statements won't keep you from overspending.

This is one of those tips I am eager to share because I spent years avoiding looking at my bank statements. I actually felt afraid to look at my bank account, looking at my bank balance and seeing how bad it looked.

That's what I wanted to avoid. I didn't want to face my bank balance because I couldn't see a way to change the situation. My unwillingness to see a way out of my financial situation created a dread in me that could have sent me spiraling down a money rabbit hole.

Fortunately, I found the courage to look at what was happening with my finances. How did I do it?

Twice a month, I made myself examine my bank statements. I conducted the reviews at the first of the month, when I paid my rent and again mid-way through the month, when I paid my other bills, expenses like my car note, car insurance, renter's insurance, and utility bills.

You might find it helpful to do the same. Set two days a month to review your bank account. In addition to spotting spending and savings trends, regular bank account reviews can help you spot cybersecurity threats.

Regularly reviewing and adjusting your bank account is just one way to grow your savings. There are a host of other ways to build your financial health. Below are steps you could take to start growing your personal savings:

- Set up an interest-bearing savings account and deposit $30 or more a month in it. Leave the money alone, not taking withdrawals, and watch the money grow.
- Pay down high interest bills like car loans, credit cards, computer loans and furniture loans as soon as possible.
- Create and stick to a budget.
- Take on a remote job working no more than 5 to 7 hours a week in addition to your full-time gig. Use the money that you earn from the job to pay off credit cards.
- Steer clear of signing adjustable rate mortgages
- Avoid taking out new loans or opening additional credit card accounts.
- Pay bills on time to avoid late fees and penalties.

If you purchase furniture and computers on 6-month or longer repayment plans, ensure that you pay off the entire balance on the purchase 30 days or more earlier than the final due date. Doing so could save you hundreds of dollars in higher interests and fees.

Set an intention to grow your savings. Look for more ways to strengthen your financial muscle. Growing savings isn't magical. It takes focus and commitment. Fortunately, you have what it takes to pull it off.

Financial Support

Open a 401K account or an Individual Retirement Arrangement (IRA) through your employer and you can gain ongoing financial support. Consider investing 6% or more of your monthly salary into the retirement accounts. As with an interest-bearing savings account, don't take withdrawals from the account. Instead, let the money grow.

Hopefully, your employer matches part of your bi-weekly retirement account investments, up to 5% or even 10%. To find out if your employer offers a retirement account, contact your human resources department. You can also learn about retirement accounts and other investment options where you work during your first week of employment, especially during open enrollment, when you set up your direct deposit and medical and dental benefits.

If you don't think investing in retirement savings through your employer is worth it, consider these examples. Should you contribute $100 a month to your retirement account and your employer contributes $10, that's $120 extra a year -- all from your employer.

Over three to five years, if you select good investments, that $120 could grow. On top of that, your retirement savings will grow based on your personal contributions. You might be shocked at how much you save over 10 years, especially if you increase your contributions as your salary grows.

Another way to get financial support is to read books that teach about smart investments, including how to grow your savings and how to make money work for you. Additionally, financial support could come through combining resources with people you know, people who are genuinely trustworthy.

For instance, when I was in the Navy and stationed in Hawaii, I tutored a boy on Saturdays. When I asked him how his family afforded to live in a large house on acres of land in Hawaii, he told me that his family pooled its resources.

To afford a large house, the boy told me that his parents, aunts, uncles, and grandparents bought and paid for the mortgage together. Even then, in my early 20s, I knew that was a clever way to build equity.

Child support is another way to get financial support. You will need a court order to get child support through the state. If your child's father balks at paying child support through an independent agreement you two made outside the court system, see if he'll agree to buy your child's clothes and shoes and pay daycare costs.

There is more than one way to get financial support for your child from your child's father. But if your child's father agrees to make certain payments, he needs to make the payment each time.

Depending on your job and passions, you might be able to tap into fellowships, grants, and other forms of financial support. If your income is low, you also might qualify to receive Section 8 to help with rent.

WIC, known as the Special Supplemental Nutrition Program for Women, Infants, and Children, might be another type of financial support you qualify to receive. Other financial support programs include the Supplemental Nutrition Assistance Program (SNAP), the Children's Health Insurance Program (CHIP), and the National School Lunch Program. Temporary Assistance for Needy Families (TANF) is another resource you could get support from. Check with local, state, and national aid programs to see if you qualify for additional support.

A local health clinic may help with prenatal care and delivery if you're pregnant and don't have medical insurance. Hospitals receive grants to help cover medical care for those in need, so you could check with your local hospital if you need financial support to cover the costs of your child's birth. You also might work out a payment plan with a hospital.

As a tip, should you apply for and receive Section 8, WIC, etc., if you want to become financially independent, set a time limit on how long you'll receive the aid.

As comfortable as it might feel to receive the aid, you'll never become financially independent this way. On top of that, your brain could create a habit where you start to believe the best you can do financially is to keep your income low and get enough aid to get by.

Something tells me that you want a lot more for your life. Receiving help is nothing to hang your head about. But to get stronger, at some point, you must develop personal financial acumen and growth.

"Prioritizing what matters most -- you and your child -- yields rewarding work decisions."

Chapter 8 – Balancing Work

Becoming a mother should be enough evidence that you are stronger than you think. It should be. However, you might be in the habit of finding fault in yourself.

Should that be the case, let me assure you that you are stronger than you think. The sooner you accept this truth, the quicker you might stop mis-prioritizing your life.

Until you accept your innate worth, an infinite worth you were created with, a worth that can never change because of what created you, mis-prioritizing what's truly important might seem like second nature.

At first glance, there might not appear to be a connection between what you believe about yourself and what you feel compelled, driven, to do. Yet, if you feel guilty or lacking in value, you might do one of four things:

- Give up, losing hope for a good life, and resigning yourself to sleeping as much as possible
- Look to others to tell you what you're worth (do this and other people's reactions will sting and hurt deeply)
- Turn yourself over to anger about how your life is going (without feeling you can improve your life)
- Convincing yourself that a bad relationship is the best you can do
- Work yourself into the ground

When you don't see your true value, you seek it everywhere. You look for it in other people's gazes and the way people let you inside their inner circle or talk to or about you.

At work, you might volunteer for special projects or complete work assignments that were initially assigned to someone else, all so you can feel valuable, worthy of another person's high perceptions and respect. Try this approach as a single mother and you could start pushing your children away, forcing them to turn to a computer tablet, cell phone or the television for communication and a makeshift babysitter.

Choose any of the remaining three options as you struggle to realize your true worth and you could spend so much time sleeping that your energy drops to the point where you don't feel like doing much, including engaging with your children. And anger is a hard emotion, an emotion that's rooted in fear, an emotion that could contaminate your entire life.

Even if you keep a watchful eye on anger, it will start to chew away at you, damaging your relationship with your child. It might start as impatience and run amok from there.

Asking others to tell you what you're worth is an endless pursuit as people's thoughts and opinions change many times during a day. Before long, you could join clubs, head social and organizational boards and take sides in arguments you don't honestly care about – all to get a head nod from people you esteem as being more valuable than you.

Each of these choices and their symptoms and effects impact you. They also impact your child.

So, value yourself. See yourself the way the Creator sees you, with infinite value. Permit yourself to receive help when needed. Avoid getting out of balance with work, pushing yourself toward working nearly nonstop. And don't try to do the work of raising your child all by yourself.

After all, being a single mom doesn't mean that you're the only person in the world. Being a single mom also doesn't mean that you must work out every step of your life on your own.

Help is around you, perhaps closer than you think.

Childcare

While your child is younger than two years old, consider partnering with a babysitter. Doing so could yield benefits.

In addition to allowing your child to be cared for in an environment that doesn't have dozens of children, taking your child to a babysitter could save you money, as daycare is not cheap.

A loving, experienced babysitter should do more than feed and hold your child. An experienced babysitter should read to your child, teach your child the alphabet, etc.

Just don't choose a babysitter only to save money. Ensure the babysitter is, indeed, experienced, loving and patient. Also, make sure that the babysitter doesn't have too many children in her care. You don't want a babysitter who's in the business solely to make money.

If you decide to partner with a daycare, shop around. Price, location, hours, licenses, and daycare workers' experience are factors to consider when shopping for a daycare.

To save yourself travel time, you might want to choose a daycare that's either close to your work or close to your home. Consider your and your child's daily schedule. You have plenty to do as a single mom. Make choices that lighten, not add to, your load.

Some employers offer onsite daycare services. This cuts down on travel, for sure. But the costs of employer daycare services could be higher than you imagine. So, check out pricing and take advantage of discounts that you could get if you pay for daycare through payroll deductions. In the United States, ChildCare.gov lists ways you could get help with paying for childcare (see the resources at the back of Thriving While Raising Happy Kids as a Single Mom for ChildCare.gov options). Outside the United States, check with your local family organizations and/or childcare agencies to familiarize yourself with support they offer.

Set Clear Work Timelines

Discuss your work schedule with your employer should you need to change your daily start and end times to care for your child or for yourself. For example, you might benefit from arriving at work an hour earlier so you can leave an hour earlier to pick your child up from the babysitter or daycare.

Perhaps the most important reasons to set clear work timelines are to:

- Ensure you get sufficient rest and relaxation each day
- Allow for time to enjoy being with your child without feeling rushed
- Set aside time to recharge and maintain healthy mental and emotional balance. Should you find yourself struggling with mental or emotional wellbeing, reach out for support from a trained, experienced, and licensed professional. Connecting with other single moms can also help. Parenting and Health Institute, One Parent, Postpartum Support International, Mums Delivery,

National Maternal Mental Health Hotline, and Single Mothers Grant, etc. are organizations that support single moms.

****

You may have heard that we teach people how to treat us. I was in my 30s when I learned this lesson and what a blessing it was to understand and accept this lesson.

To better manage your day and teach others what you need to balance parenting with work, set clear work timelines with your children and extended family by:

- Letting your children know what time you must leave for work and when you will be home from work
- Sticking to work start and end times (even if you work from home)
- Making it clear to friends and family when you have time to travel, vacation, etc.
- Prioritize work assignments, completing top priority projects first
- Making good use of time management tools like digital assistant apps, upgraded software, wireless headsets so you can knock out telephone calls while cooking, working on projects, etc.
- Reminding family of your start and end workday times. You may have to do this several times if you work from home.
- Waking in time to commute to work without rushing
- Communicate instances when your time is tight, reducing opportunities for you to do favors for others

Also, just because people ask you to do favors, run errands, drive them to different places, doesn't mean that you must. Your time is limited as a single mom. Don't run yourself ragged trying to please people. In addition to raising one or more children, you may have a full-time job. Depending on your situation, you could be working two or more jobs.

As you set clear work timelines, before long, people will become familiar with your work schedule. They'll know when you're generally in for the evening and might not ask you for favors after that evening hour arrives.

Older children will become familiar with your work hours. They'll know what time you generally sit down and relax for the evening. This applies even if you work remotely.

Furthermore, as it regards remote work, it's especially important that you set clear work timelines, and not with other people – with yourself. If you don't create clear work timelines with yourself, you could end up working 12 or more hours a day, putting yourself in a state of continual stress and fatigue.

Powerful Communication

Want to be heard? Want to be understood?

Communicate clearly. Let the people in your life know where and when you need to be somewhere. Also, let them know when you need time, space, and quiet to focus on a goal, ways to deepen your relationship with your child or time to map out an upcoming work initiative.

As a tip, if you're like me and you worry about what other people think about you, to communicate clearly, you might have to work at it. Why? If you worry about what people think about you, you could fall into the trap of doing what others ask you to do even if you don't want to do what's asked of you.

Another choice you might make is to repress your desires so you can be more aware of another person's requests. Let this develop into a habit and you could be a prime candidate for burnout or depression.

Why? Your true desires are there . . . inside you. Repressing or ignoring them does not change or erase your authentic desires. Instead, repressing or ignoring your true desires creates disappointment, disillusionment, and heartache. None of these is empowering, so you don't need them.

To stop worrying about what others think:

- Remind yourself that you don't know what another person is thinking. In fact, you probably don't know what you're thinking at the subconscious level.

- Love yourself. Focus on your innate good. Celebrate recent successes.
- Read scripture and other writings that echo how the Creator created you.

Because you'll hear comments from different people and get a range of expressions from others, take daily actions to strengthen yourself so you stop worrying about what others are thinking. The less concern you have for another's perceptions, the easier it will be to communicate clearly.

Parenting effectively requires clear communication. Regarding parenting, you'll need clear communication to:

- Let your child's father know when you need him to pick your child up and return your child home
- Tell a friend that you don't have the bandwidth to keep their child this weekend
- Inform your employer that you must leave early to attend your child's school play, sports event, etc.
- Remove any confusion from your child's mind about their bedtime and when they should prepare for school

The more consistently you send clear communications, the better. Communicate clearly and you won't have to repeat yourself. These factors could aid your communications:

- Know why you want to share a message
- Consider your audience. Talking with a child often requires more basic language. And some adults and children listen better when you communicate with images, use shorter sentences, etc.

- Incorporate nonverbal cues into your message
- Sharpen your emotional intelligence
- Prepare what you want to say ahead of time when conveying important messages
- Try a message out on a friend. See if they know what you're saying or if they get confused
- Don't expect people to read your mind

Whatever you communicate, if you want to be taken seriously, keep your word. Do what you say you will. Give people time to meet your requests if you're asking for a favor, etc.

Also, be kind and considerate. This applies whether you're communicating over the phone, in writing or in-person. Keep what you want to convey top of mind. Never make hurting someone the goal.

Be Disciplined

"Your word is all you have." I can't count how many times I heard that when I was growing up. My paternal grandparents and my father told me that.

Their message made it clear that it was very important that I keep my word, that I do what I had said I would. Years later, I would see the value in what they shared.

The saying impacts so much. For instance, money comes and goes. Moods that you experience change. Appearance alters. These are changes that you might not always be able to control.

However, keeping your word -- doing what you say you will do -- is within your grasp. If you say you're going to attend your child's track and field meet, show up. If you say you're going to attend your child's school play, show up. If you say you're going to be more patient with your child, do so. If you say you're going to stop engaging in a bad habit, stop the habit.

If you say you're going to read to your child at bedtime, do so. Keep your word. Doing so teaches your child to do what she says she will do. It places value on what is said.

Believe it or not, raising your child is an area where you might be tempted to make promises that you won't deliver on. This is because you want your child to feel happiness. So, you might promise your child that you'll buy toys, video games, clothes, and concert tickets that you know they want.

Seeing your child's face light up with excitement and anticipation is rewarding. This experience can fill you with happiness, not after you give your child what you promised, but now.

Yet, if you don't keep your promise, if you don't keep your word, your child will be disappointed, maybe even sad. If this keeps happening, the wound cuts deeper.

This is why you might prefer to choose not to make promises to your child. Instead of making promises, you could tell your child that you need time to think through what's being asked of you.

Keeping your word at work, in the community, at school and at social engagements you attend sends a message that you can be trusted. Living a disciplined life and keeping your word also builds trust in yourself.

It takes discipline to keep your word. It takes discipline not to make promises you aren't certain that you can keep. It takes discipline to map out and build the life you want you and your child to live.

"Strong foundations withstand lots of shifts and weightiness."

Chapter 9 – Strong Support

Have the courage to seek support when you need it. Though often repeated, this cannot be uttered too much. You're a single mom, but you're not meant to live your life or raise your child alone.

Building and accessing a strong support system helps you to recharge, not every now and then but regularly. A strong support system can also give your children other kids to play and develop social skills with.

For instance, if two friends, a cousin and a colleague are part of your support system and these people have children, those kids could become ready-made friends for your child. Let that be the case and while your friend is looking after your child while you're at a doctor's appointment, watching your child could be easy simply because your friend's kids keep your child busy having fun at play.

That's just two benefits your strong support system can offer. Perhaps more importantly is a team of people to share challenges with, talking and working through obstacles together.

Even if you have a strong mind and have pushed your way through a lot of challenging experiences, you're going to need people to lean on as a single mom. So, don't shut yourself off.

As a pastor at a church I attended shared, "To have a friend, be a friend." It might help if you recall the way you made friends when you were a kid.

Back then, you probably spoke to kids in the neighborhood you lived in, not once a day, but every time you saw them. You might have waved and spoken to kids in the neighborhood even if they were new to the area and you hadn't seen them before.

Try doing the same now. Strike up a conversation with a new, trustworthy neighbor or colleague. Instead of telling yourself every relationship is going to turn out poorly, consider believing that a few new relationships might turn out very good.

When colleagues invite you to lunch or to a ball game, consider taking them up on the offer. Other ways to make friends and build a strong support system include:

- Joining a book club, a great choice if you love to learn and/or love reading books for entertainment
- Participate in a social group at a nature center
- Volunteer at an organization that supports people in your community who are in need
- Participate in the local Chamber of Commerce
- Be active in a volunteer orchestra, band, theater group, etc.

Also, online organizations like Meetup include women's groups that you could join. Some of these groups take cruises, visit wineries, go horseback riding, attend movies together and travel abroad.

During inclement weather you could gain support by attending webinars and virtual events that allow you to connect and speak with other single moms, women entrepreneurs and women who are active in the community. Just ensure that many of your interactions with others are in-person.

Connecting with people, especially in-person, getting outdoors, exercising, investing in a healthy diet, and sleeping deeply at night will pay off hugely. So, get out there! Develop new rewarding relationships and keep relationships with friends and family open and strong.

Family Near and Far

Although this chapter may seem like an echo of the previous chapter, it isn't. Five generations ago, your parents, sisters, brothers, aunts, uncles, cousins and even your distant relatives likely would have lived in the same town you lived in.

Back then, grandparents and great-grandparents didn't go to a nursing home. Families lived together. They looked out for each other. If you've seen *The Waltons*, you got a glimpse of how families cared for each other generations earlier.

Airplanes, work arrangements and the rate at which people move to different neighborhoods, cities and states has made it hard for a lot of families to look out for each other the way families once did. To land higher paying jobs sometimes relatives are required to move out of state.

Fortunately, just as technology has assisted families in the change from being homesteads to spreading across thousands of miles, expanding into retail, hospitality, education, entertainment and sports, technology is helping families who live states and countries apart to keep in touch. Whether you live near your parents, brothers, sisters, and other relatives, consider making it a priority to keep the relationship you share with your relatives healthy and strong.

There are many ways to do this. You can call at least one relative each week. Additionally, you can text relatives weekly or monthly. Write family birthdays on a wall calendar and send birthday cards, gifts, or flowers to say "Happy Birthday" to relatives.

Should trustworthy relatives ask to babysit, take them up on the offer. Doing so will show you that you have more help than you might have thought.

Circle of Friends

Surround yourself with a circle of friends. Don't tell yourself that the best is behind you should you be a single mom because you divorced, or your husband transitioned.

There's so much good ahead.

Your circle of friends should grow naturally. As your circle expands, shifts, diminishes, and grows again, celebrate friends who share your family make-up. Yes.

Welcome single moms into your circle of friends. You may meet these women through work, a community event or a relative. Because motherhood is a lifelong journey, it's a blessing to share hard times, celebrations, and great forward strides that you or your child experience with other mothers.

Community, family, friends, and faith are messages repeated in this book. Why? You cannot have too much of these.

You're going to have a host of experiences. You can get through them all. However, some may rock your confidence, possibly pushing you toward fear.

If you're raising your child 75% or more totally on your own without the support of family, the child's father or friends, there will be days and nights when you'll feel absolutely exhausted. Here are tips to help with fatigue:

- Put your infant in bed around the same time at night. This could help your child become accustomed to falling asleep at a certain time.

- Keep your child active three to four hours before bedtime, allowing your child's body to tire naturally, welcoming sleep.
- Retire to bed around the same time at night yourself. This helps to train your brain to start to prepare for sleep.
- Turn off technology before you climb into bed.
- Enjoy a cup of noncaffeinated tea two hours before going to bed.
- Exercise regularly for 45 minutes to an hour a day.
- Eat and drink a healthy diet.
- Avoid eating heavy meals four hours before bedtime.
- Jot down activities that pop into your mind at night, things you want to complete the next day, allowing you to let the thoughts go after you write them down so you can enjoy a good night of sleep.
- Spend at least an hour a day outdoors in a safe environment. Vitamin D helps produce melatonin, which is a natural sleep aid.
- Try eating cherries and/or drinking organic cherry juice (cherries have natural melatonin)
- Journal about situations that concern you. It might surprise you how writing about what's worrying you reduces the worry.

Get in the habit of letting your mind start to relax as evening approaches. If something is still bothering you after taking three or more of the above actions, consider talking with a friend. Get outside your head. Talking with a friend can help you see a situation differently.

Perceiving a situation differently, in a less stressful way, is part of what happens during therapy, not that you should put the weight of being your therapist on a friend. You shouldn't, but talking with a good friend can help you see a relationship, a work situation, parenting, or a stage your child is going through differently, in a way that lets you see that you can successfully get through what you're facing.

Give your friend space to share anything that's worrying them with you. After all, that's what friends do. They help each other. And they acknowledge and celebrate wins.

Worship Centers

If you appreciate acknowledging blessings you have received, discovering more about the Creator, and connecting with likeminded people, attending, or joining a worship center inhabited by inwardly healthy people (not all people who attend worship centers are inwardly healthy) might prove to be a significant blessing, not just now but over the rest of your physical journey.

Should you decide to attend a worship center, consider visiting first. Visit with an open mind, not expecting anything magical to happen.

If you're visiting a small worship center, don't be surprised if members eagerly welcome you. It's not uncommon for members of small churches to be excited to see newcomers. Members might even invite you to join leadership boards and auxiliaries at the church, organizations like the Missionary Society, Hospitality Society, Pastor's Aide Society or Youth Club.

Larger worship centers are big enough to slip inside and enjoy a sermon without too many people, if anyone, noticing you as a new arrival. Yet, even if you want to attend worship services mostly unnoticed, connecting with other worshippers may be the best way to thrive at a worship center.

Just make sure that you don't volunteer for projects right away or join two or more leadership boards or auxiliaries. After all, you're not attending a worship center to add to your workload. If you do join a worship center and people, including influential church members, start asking you to join organizations and take on work, consider saying "No" if doing so will add to your already demanding schedule.

In other words, if joining an auxiliary will add an hour or more a week to your schedule, think twice before accepting the offer. Don't join a worship center, a committee at a worship center or take on projects at church to make someone else feel good.

Despite how they might appear or carry themselves, people who attend worship centers are human beings, no different than you. They are not special people as no one is special.

So, avoid taking on projects that push you into overload. After all, being a single mom gives you more than enough to do. If you do regularly attend a worship center, benefits you could gain include:

- Opportunities to connect with people who share your faith and beliefs
- Youth programs your child might love being a part of
- Kids for your child to play and grow up with
- Weekend events to have fun at (e.g., cookouts, festivals, trips to fellowship with other churches)
- People to become friends with

Joining a church was one of the best decisions that I made as a single mom. I was fortunate to join a church where members were so loving that visiting churches were surprised at the love they felt when they entered the sanctuary.

In addition to there being other single mothers at the church, the pastor and church leaders supported all the church's members, regardless of their marital status. My son had fun playing with other kids at church.

I even found a babysitter there, an older woman who attended the church. To this day, I remain in contact with people from that church although I live in a different state and have for several years.

Looking back, I wonder how things would have gone for me while I raised my son as a single mom if I hadn't connected with that worship center. I don't think I would have felt as much a part of the community or that I had someone nearby to call on should I face an emergency. This was important for me because none of my relatives lived in the state that I did.

Take your time deciding which worship center to join. Pray about it and trust that you'll receive the right guidance. If at any time you don't feel comfortable at a specific church or other worship center, remember that you have options.

Choose the right worship center for you and your child. And know that throughout your attendance at a worship center, you and your child should feel comfortable, safe, and welcomed. You and your child should feel loved.

Volunteer

Performing outreach can keep you from focusing on your many responsibilities which could, in turn, protect you from entering a state of overwhelm.

Choose volunteer work that won't burden you. For example, you could tutor someone for an hour a month. Other ways to volunteer include:

- Reading to students at the school your child attends
- Volunteering as a chaperon on a trip at your child's school
- Assisting at a library
- Conducting volunteer work at a hospital or clinic
- Helping to clean trash up in the community you live in
- Packing books to ship to in-need schools

A volunteer project I took up as a single mom was to help compile student book bags and school materials for kids in need. It was during this project that I saw more clearly how poorly far too many children are treated in their family homes.

Although I grew up in rough housing projects, my eyes were opened. My heart went out to the kids who grew up in dysfunctional homes. Was I ever happy to purchase and help organize school supplies, stocking new book bags with the supplies, giving children in-need the chance to start school with basic school materials.

Other forms of volunteer work I did show me the importance of being there for youth and adults in need.

Volunteering also helps volunteers to see how much room for improvement there is in the communities where they live.

Although there are benefits to be gained from volunteering, avoid volunteering because you want to save someone, a community, or the world. Instead, volunteer to engage in outreach.

Again, outreach keeps you from zoning in on yourself. It helps you to see the challenges, wins and everyday ups and downs everyone deals with.

"Challenges single moms face stir a great inner strength."

Chapter 10 – When It Gets Hard

By the time your child reaches adulthood, you'll be as strong as any superwoman. You'll have had a myriad of experiences that push, stretch, and outright challenge you to the core.

There may be times when you wish that you could roll back the clock and become a child again yourself. It wouldn't be a surprise if you started to feel this way after you've been juggling a dozen or more responsibilities (e.g., feeding your baby, driving your child to daycare, commuting to and from work, preparing meals, working seven to nine hours a day, playing with your child, exercising).

Juggle a dozen or more responsibilities, activities you must complete, at the least, every weekday for six months and you could start to wear down physically, mentally, and emotionally. Forget feeling embarrassed, guilty, or ashamed for feeling tired.

You're not alone. There are many single moms who feel this way. Practicing awareness may help you avoid burnout and overwhelm.

What's meant by "practicing awareness" is simply paying attention to how you're feeling and thinking. In other words, become aware of what's going on in your inner world.

It's much better to become "aware" of the fact that you're feeling unusually stressed or that you have been falling into bed exhausted for more than four consecutive days than it is to ignore these inner shifts. After all, the sooner you become aware of these non-optimal shifts within yourself, the sooner you can start to make changes.

Within this chapter, we'll discuss situations that might feel particularly difficult. We'll also present actions you could take to shift out of a difficult situation.

Get Still

Juggling a hectic schedule isn't the only thing that can create a sense of overwhelm. A tight financial situation, an illness, fights with your child's father and arguments with your child's grandparents, including your own parents can push you into overwhelm.

If your child raising techniques are different from your parents or even your older siblings, don't be surprised if you get push back. Should the push back and criticisms continue, you could start to feel stressed.

Pay attention to how you're feeling. Catch yourself early and you could avoid slipping into overwhelm.

One more thing before we discuss actions you could take to avoid or to counter overwhelm. And it's this -- as odd as it sounds, slipping into constant overwhelm could cause being overwhelmed to feel "normal".

It's similar to how you might think "hollering" while you're upset is normal if you grew up in a home where your caretakers hollered at each other when they felt angry. The downside to normalizing feeling "overwhelmed" is that, once you normalize a state of being, you could get stuck in the state.

This happened to me. It snuck up on me, in part, because I thought it was normal to feel overwhelmed every day as a single mom. Before I knew it, more than six years had passed, and I hadn't seen a butterfly. I also rarely heard birds singing or saw squirrels playing in trees.

It took me years to pull out of this state, but I was committed and kept trying different techniques (many which are shared in Thriving While Raising Happy Kids as a Single Mom) until I shifted out of overwhelm. It is my aim to help you avoid slipping into overwhelm, depression, or a sense of helplessness.

This first technique is simple and could be implemented nearly anywhere. If you're pressed for time and rushing, take five to ten seconds to sit still and breathe deeply.

So, let's say you're feeling exhausted, angry, frustrated, or hopeless. Sit still for a few seconds, focusing on your breath, until you start to feel the fear-based emotion lower. I've even gone into a public bathroom stall and sat; it works.

Consider this a quick technique to use when you're in emotional tight spots. For example, you could sit still and breathe deeply *before* you talk with your child about a poor grade or about a note your child's teacher sent home about your child's behavior.

Although the technique can be used nearly anywhere, to enter and maintain a healthy mental, emotional, and physical state of being, make sitting still for 10 to 15 minutes a day a part of every morning and every evening.

Depending on what's going on in your life, it might be beneficial to sit still during the afternoon too. To do this, simply sit on your sofa, the edge of your bed, your porch, or another location that you naturally feel peaceful being in.

Allow thoughts to pass like clouds floating across the sky. Steer clear of attaching labels or judgments to thoughts that cross your mind. Simply let the thoughts come and go.

While you do this, breathe. Just breathe.

Breathe in.

Breathe out.

Relax.

Breathe in.

Breathe out.

Relax.

Sit still in the morning and again at night just before you go to bed. This simple technique can yield remarkable results.

Call Your Sister

Time is another factor that can push you into states of overwhelm as a single mom. That's right. Time.

In fact, if you grew up being repeatedly told how important it is to never be late, to always "be on time", staying on time to work meetings, parent-teacher conferences, your child's sports events, etc. can start to feel like a "thing" that is pushing you too hard. A first step toward freeing yourself from the bounds of time is to review your perceptions about time.

Points to consider as you review your perceptions about time are:

- Do you feel as if you're "good" if you arrive at events "on time"?
- Is showing up late a sign of disrespect to you?
- How were you treated as a child when you were late or did something that caused your parents to be late?

Next, look at the perceptions. Are they true? (Perceptions are never 100% accurate.) Are there any perceptions that you would benefit from changing? Which ones? What specific actions can you take to start changing those perceptions?

Years ago, I stopped wearing a watch. Another thing I did was to stop asking people to tell me what time it was. And I stopped looking for clocks so I could check the time. It did tremendous good, lifting pressure around what time it was from me. I appreciate having taken that choice to this day.

Whatever you decide to do, write those specific actions down. It may help to hold you accountable for completing the actions.

You could also discuss your perceptions about time and how you can free yourself from being bound to time with your sister. If you don't have a sister, build rewarding relationships with girlfriends.

Although there's no need to tell your sister everything that you're experiencing or planning, share some things with her. This is a woman who's proven herself trustworthy, someone who truly loves and cares about you. She might be your biological sister and she might be a woman you met who isn't related to you.

The choice is certainly yours. However, prioritizing "keeping secrets" could set you up for heartache. When you prioritize keeping secrets, responsibilities get heavy. Opportunities to see an issue differently, allowing you to find a solution, are diminished.

Questions, ideas, worries and solutions that fill your mind are almost always your own when you make "keeping secrets" a priority. Life feels burdensome then. Plus, keeping secrets is weighty all by itself.

Humans are communicators. If you're always careful about what you say for fear that you might disclose a secret, you could be keeping an important secret from yourself. That secret could be that you either think you're not enough or that you think you're inferior to others.

In other words, you might want to prevent others from becoming aware of facts about you because you think others would see you negatively. If you're honest with yourself, you might see that there are facts about you that you're embarrassed about.

A sister can help you let that go. Also, as your sister helps you to free yourself of the erroneous belief that you're less than anyone else or that you need to keep secrets because there are facts about you that are an embarrassment – you help your sister.

As you trust your sister more, she may start to trust you more. This opens you both up to the chance to deepen friendships and have a trustworthy person to discuss challenges and worries with. It also gives you both someone to share successes and forward paths with.

Pray and Trust

It's unfortunate that we spend so much time thinking about the "future", a time that never comes. However, not only do we throw away "the present" when we focus on the future, we often catastrophize simple things, expecting bad things to happen to us in the future.

Don't engage in this bad habit if you want to live a good life. Just because your child's teacher may have sent a note requesting to meet with you to discuss your child's academic performance or behavior doesn't mean that your child is about to get suspended.

In fact, your child's teacher might want to tell you that they think your child should be tested to see if your child qualifies to be in a gifted class. Regarding a note requesting to meet with you to discuss your child's behavior, the teacher might want to tell you that they've noticed your child often plays alone during breaks in school.

Talking with your child to discover if anyone is bothering them could resolve the issue. Or you might see good results after you give your child tips on fun ways to build self-confidence and start making new, caring friends.

Even if you take this approach, watch yourself. If you've spent years catastrophizing, you might be relieved that your child isn't bullying another kid or disrupting class only to, seconds later, start worrying that your child is unhappy or could potentially be dealing with an emotional or mental health issue.

Be intentional when it comes to putting an end to trying to live in the future. Catch yourself early and tell yourself that your focus is on what's happening NOW. Also, set an intention to count your blessings.

Start looking for what's good in your life. Set aside time every day to look for and count your blessings. Now, you're developing better daily habits with these two intentions.

Prayer is another activity to add to your day. If you're not in the habit of praying, it may take a while to see the value in daily prayer.

Pray for yourself. Pray for your child. Pray for whatever matters to you. Pray for guidance, insight, and wisdom. When you pray specific prayers, consider writing the prayer down and then watch what happens.

Although prayer isn't magic, when you power prayer with faith, you will get results. The combination of prayer and faith can give you hope.

Talk to Another Single Mother

If you're the only single mom whose life situation is like yours, there's a chance that you could feel alone. You might even feel isolated.

Fortunately, there's lots of help. At the top of the help options are other single moms. Even if you haven't met a woman who's raising a child singlehandedly, there's bound to be another single mom in the town you live in.

There might be local organizations that support single parents where you live. Through these organizations, you could learn about networking events, tutoring opportunities, daycares, and grants as well as ways to save on diapers, clothes, and education.

Another single mom can also give you insight into companies that offer flexible schedules to support working parents. Should you be in the market for a new job, another single mom might tell you about an employment opportunity that you'll love.

Talking with another single mom is also a great way to compare notes as it regards potty training, teaching your child to read, count and write and helping your child develop strong social skills. You can lean on each other when either of you feel stressed.

Because both of you are having similar experiences, you already know the types of situations you're both dealing with. Your children might become good friends. Most of all, you'll have someone to confide in and express yourself to who understands what you face from day-to-day.

Should you need additional support, consider working with an experienced, reputable, licensed psychotherapist. If you work with a therapist who raised a child solo, you might build a bridge with the therapist that makes it easier to allow your subconscious to heal.

If you're dealing with depression, you might find articles like Coping with Depression as a Single Mom | Psych Central and Single Parenting Stress: How to Beat Burnout (verywellmind.com) helpful.

Your local telephone book lists licensed therapists. Your employer might also offer free mental health support through an Employee Assistance Program. Mental Health America, Wealthy Single Mommy, and National Child and & Maternal Health are other organizations that offer support for single moms.

Journaling Helps

There may be times when talking about what you're going through with another person doesn't feel right. And there might be instances when you don't feel open to even praying and verbalizing what you're going through. This is when you might want to try journaling.

Journaling could help you to express your thoughts, feelings, and concerns. You don't need a special journal. Simply sit down and start writing about what you're dealing with and what you plan to do to get through the challenge.

Write about how you felt when the challenge started to develop. Put pen to paper and write down how you tried (or didn't try) to stop the event from happening. Really dig in on what's happening and especially what you think about what is happening. Also, dig into what you're feeling.

Believe it or not, this is a great way to work through what's troubling you. Keep at it. See if you don't feel better after you write in your journal.

Years later, you could go back and read over previous journal entries and see how you've grown and changed. Another thing you could do is to spot recurring themes in your life. Once you spot recurring themes, you could zone in on solutions to stop engaging in habits that hold you back.

If you're working to free yourself from the habit of making it a priority to keep secrets, writing in a journal will allow you to share what's going on with you, to get it out, without telling another person. Should you choose this route, while you're getting in the habit of journaling make sure that you connect with other people. Don't isolate or build barriers around yourself, keeping other people at bay.

"Fill yourself with love, enough to pour goodness into your child."

Chapter 11 – What About You

Raising a child takes 18 or more years. There may be times when you'll devote your entire life to your child, depending on the situation. But this shouldn't become the norm unless your child has special needs. You and your child aren't the same person. You have a life, and you need to develop and invest in your life, blooming and expanding in joy, love, and wonder.

There's a part of you that wants to be cared for. Countering that is a part of you that believes in the value of sacrifice, namely putting yourself behind someone else, anyone else.

If you ignore your desire to be cared for, the end could find you facing regret. A part of you will feel unloved – by you.

Are you accustomed to feeling as if you're loving yourself as you push yourself too hard and sacrifice your joy to allow another person to have what they want? If you've become accustomed to *choosing* to put yourself last, the following words might feel flat and empty, but they're not.

It is crucial that you love yourself. Although your consciousness might wave aside the need to love yourself, the call to do so won't silence. Forego loving yourself and your subconscious mind might start sending you unignorable messages.

Make this a priority. Consider yourself.

What causes you to feel joy, loved, cared for, valued, and happy? Do you love listening to smooth jazz, country, rhythm and blues, rock, or classical music? Do you love to dance, swim, sing, paint, work with crafts, write or put puzzles together?

Do you love to travel, visit museums, and learn, try different cuisines, soak in a warm bubble bath or work in theater? How often do you engage in these activities?

Why not start making room in your life for what you love? The payoff will be huge if you do at least three things each day that cause you to feel loved, cared for and valued.

Design Your Beautiful Life

Yes. Your days are full, at times overflowing with activity. Still – this is your life, and you deserve to design and live a beautiful life. But the beautiful life you deserve to live isn't going to come together on its own.

Whether you pray, sit still, meditate, go for nature walks, and wait for an answer to surface into your consciousness from the Creator, you have a part to play in your life's design.

Start from the inside. When you consider your inner world what do you want? Do you want more peace, more time to sit down and relax, more happiness, more confidence, more patience and to have your spiritual eyes opened so you can start to truly know yourself and what you really want?

Take several days to consider what you want your inner world to look like. Really take your time to think about your inner world.

Next, consider your outer or physical world. How is your health? Would you like to improve your health by eating or drinking food and beverages that fuel your body with valuable vitamins and minerals?

Are you happy with your living situation? Is your apartment, house, hut, teepee, or camper in a safe neighborhood, the type of neighborhood you're happy to call home? Is your child growing up in the physical environment that you want them to?

If you'd like to see changes, how will you cause these changes to show up in your physical world? Are you curious about how to design a life you love?

There are books that outline steps you could take to get from where you are now to where you want to be. Among these books, there's:

- Awaken The Giant Within by Anthony Robbins
- In The Meantime by Iyanla Vanzant
- Breaking The Habit of Being Yourself by Joe Dispenza
- Creating Your Best Life by Caroline Miller
- Atomic Habits by James Clear
- Better Than Before by Gretchen Rubin
- The Power of Positive Thinking by Norman Vincent Peale
- You Are A Badass by Jen Sincero
- Live Your Dreams by Les Brown

Opening Your Heart

Your child sees you working hard, caring for them, paying expenses and taking care of your home, whether you live in an apartment, house, camper, or another dwelling. Isn't it time to let your child see you happy, not every now and then but every day?

Even more, why not let your child sometimes join you when you do what you love, something that opens your heart? This might teach your child to prioritize ensuring that joy is always in their life.

Can your child and you paint together? Can you two have a blast creating a play that you could perform for your family, including cousins, nieces, nephews, and other relatives?

Let your child suggest activities that you both love. You may learn so much about each other as you start engaging in activities that open your heart. Use the following pages to list fun things you love to do, actions that easily open your heart to more good.

_____

_____

_____

_____

_____

_____

_____

_____

_____

_____

Fun Is Part of Thriving

Piggybacking on doing what you love is the importance of fueling life with fun. Like many things in this world, fueling your life with fun won't *just happen*. To add fun to each day, you need to be intentional.

Similar to how you are intentional about preparing breakfast, exercising, taking your child to school or watching a favorite TV show, it's time to become intentional about having fun. Choose games that are fun and educational, and you could strengthen your child's and your learning.

MindWare, Prodigy, Coko Games and Geek Galore Games are just a few resources where you could find online and offline games. There are games for children, teens, and adults. You could get games by subject, holiday, or season.

Baking cookies, making vegetable smoothies, playing musical instruments, building puzzles, drawing in coloring books and water painting are activities your child and you could have fun with. Watching your and your child's favorite sports team in action can also be great fun.

Writing this brings back sweet memories of my son and me watching the Philadelphia 76ers on TV and in-person (back when Allen Iverson played for the 76ers). Did we ever have fun! During the Eastern Conference Finals, I even jumped up and down on the bed cheering for the 76ers.

Talk about feeling like a kid again! My son was surprised to see me jumping up and down on the bed. We had so much fun! Looking back, I see that it was fun experiences like that that deepened the bond my son and I shared. Around that time, I became increasingly committed to adding fun things to my son and my days.

But don't force it. Do things your child and you are interested in, activities that are connected to what you love. For instance, if your child and you love being outdoors in nature, you could go for a hike in a safe area with friends.

Other fun nature activities include swimming, collecting seashells, creating a scrapbook filled with colorful autumn leaves and tending to a flower garden. Riding a bike around your neighborhood and watching and identifying different types of birds and butterflies are other things your child and you could do to fuel your days with fun.

Three Things

What would your life look and feel like if, for every responsibility you fulfilled that you didn't enjoy completing, you followed it up by doing three activities you love? You could even schedule the responsibility you didn't want to complete on a day when your schedule isn't already jammed with one thing after another to do.

This is going to take creativity. You're going to have to search your past and present, searching for activities you've loved engaging in. As the days pass, you may need to think about movies, TV shows, cartoons, etc. you've seen. What happened in these media forms that struck you as funny, exciting, or fun?

How can you add these events to your life? As you search for things you love to do, your brain starts focusing on good experiences. Use the below space to jot down three deliverables you don't like. Follow those three up with three activities you love. Revisit the prior section to pull over several fun activities.

Chore #1: _____

_____

Fun Choice #1: _____

_____

Fun Choice #2: _____

_____

Fun Choice #3: _____

_____

Chore #2 _____

_____

Fun Choice #1: _____

_____

Fun Choice #2: _____

_____

Fun Choice #3: _____

_____

Chore #3 _____

_____

Fun Choice #1: _____

_____

Fun Choice #2: _____

_____

Fun Choice #3: _____

_____

_____

"Change instant by instant into someone remarkable, the woman you always knew you were."

Chapter 12 – Shifts and Changes

There are life events that highlight change. Births, transitions, job shifts, home relocations, anniversaries, weddings, and graduations are obvious major life changes. It's these life events that draw family and friends around you.

You've already seen this in action. People who love you were happy to catch planes, walk or drive to your home to greet your newborn baby.

Your excitement seems to spill over into these people. They come to your or your child's graduation with balloons, flowers, and gifts. Anniversaries and birthdays are celebrated at banquet halls, restaurants and an aunt's or grandparents' residence.

It's as if shifts and changes are symbols of good. But if that's the case, why is it so hard to progress through major life events?

You're not alone if you dislike encountering change. A lot of people dislike change. Change signals a loss of control. It also sends you into uncertainty. When there's a shift, you don't know what's coming next.

If change thrusts you into a different environment, your brain will have to adjust. This is a process that could take months. While you're adjusting to one major shift (e.g., birth, family member transitioning, graduation) more major or minor changes could be occurring.

There's another key area where you are bound to experience shifts and changes, and that is with raising your child. Keep reading to discover strategies you could implement to progress through shifts and changes that are specific to single parenting.

Childhood to Adulthood – So Much Change

Because you were the center of the change that you experienced as an infant and growing child, you probably don't remember the countless shifts you went through from the cradle to being a single mom. What you won't forget are the shifts and changes you witness your child going through.

You won't forget how the changes your child experiences affect your life. Do any of these sound familiar?

- How surprised you felt the first time your child slept through the entire night
- Seeing your child's first tooth come in
- Hearing your child say "Mama", "Mommy", "Maman", "Mahsi", "Mother" or "Mom" for the first time
- Watching your child let go of the table edge and take off walking on their own
- Your child walking into school for first grade without you

You might fill up with surprise, excitement and pride as each event occurs. At a certain point, and as the changes continue, mixed in with surprise, excitement and pride might be fear.

You might feel reluctant to see your child go through more and more major shifts. Why? Each shift that your child goes through is evidence that you're changing too.

Once your child enters high school you might start to notice that your hair is greying, even if you only see a few grey hairs. And inflammation might start to cause your joints to stiffen, even if only slightly.

That's right. You're getting older just as your child is aging. You're changing and maturing too. These tips on dealing with change might help you progress through shifts and changes:

- Practice awareness to spot signs of upcoming change early, giving yourself time to adjust to what's coming
- Talk with others who have already progressed through the type of change you're facing
- Be patient with yourself and your child, as everyone handles change differently
- Focus on your life priorities
- Bring blessings and things you appreciate front and center
- Take full responsibility for your life
- Accept that you cannot control life
- See if you can spot goodness in the change
- Stick to a healthy daily routine
- Practice self-care

Unexpected Experiences

Before you know it, your child's personality will blossom. If your child was inquisitive and outgoing as a toddler, they might become quieter and more contemplative as they get older or vice versa.

Your child's circle of friends will likely change the older your child gets. Don't be shocked if you don't care for one or more of your child's friends. You might even wonder what it is about those people that your child likes so much.

On top of the above, when you connect with other single moms you might hear about unexpected experiences they've had with their child. For instance, you might hear that:

- After struggling with a physical ailment, a child is becoming an athletic phenom
- A child who once performed well in school has become withdrawn and their grades are suffering
- Although often seen laughing, a child has been bullied and kept it a secret for years
- An adult child who had spent several months in and out of rehab has been sober for more than four years
- Whereas video games once occupied the majority of a child's after school attention, socializing with caring friends now takes up most of the child's free time

Prepare yourself. Despite how much time and energy you invest in your child, your child will undergo experiences that surprise you, changes you simply do not expect to occur.

Keep connecting with other single moms and talking with your own mother, aunts, sisters, friends, and grandmothers – women who may have walked in the shoes you're now wearing.

Watching a Human Bloom

By now you have seen that you're more than a precious child's mother, you're watching a human bloom. Another way to look at it is to acknowledge that you're being gifted with the blessing to witness the miracle of a human life opening and expanding into magnificent brilliance.

Not only that, as a single mom, you're an influencer, having tremendous impact on the way that a human life expands and awakens. Single mom, you're in a place of unimaginable power!

Gift your child with the freedom to bloom into who she or he truly is. Gift yourself by raising, nurturing, and supporting someone who celebrates, dances, is at peace with and lives in the joy of who they truly are.

This means that you give your child space (and loving permission) to be authentic. You don't force your child to work tirelessly to experience worldly success in a sport, academic, scientific, arts, nature, or other space that you always wanted to enjoy huge success with but haven't.

Also, don't force your child to pursue a career, degree, or another goal that you think will help your child to make more money than you made, help your child to simply pay housing costs or help your child to compete or compare well against their peers. Forcing your child to go down paths that push your child away from authenticity may feel good to you but will likely cause your child tremendous pain now or later.

Here's the trick. You might be *forcing* your child to go down a path and not even know it. So, here's a tip. Signs that you're forcing your child to move away from authenticity include:

- Not fully listening to your child when he tells you about an interest that he has that you don't want him to engage in (it could be sports, engineering, law enforcement, etc.)
- Frowning when you see your child doing something you don't like, something that isn't harmful in any way
- Celebrating each time your child says or does what you want them to
- Repeatedly announcing achievements made by a sibling, a child in the neighborhood or a child of a friend, etc. in an area you wish your child would get more involved with and perform better in

A tremendous benefit you gain when you let your child bloom authentically is to watch your child grow up with confidence, courage, strength, peace, and joy. These blessings are infectious. They will impact you and everyone your child meets.

After your child reaches adulthood, she will likely appreciate that you had the courage to allow her to become who she truly is, that you supported her journey from childhood to adulthood. In fact, your child might thank you for this verbally and non-verbally for the rest of her physical journey.

To repeat, it takes courage to let go and allow the Creator to guide your child to where your child should be. So, use your courage. It's worth it.

Consider how many people your child has met. Then, think about the people your child could meet years from now. Your courage to allow your child to bloom is going to impact each person your child meets. Do what it takes to let that impact be good.

Patience Matters

Patience is a lesson you will learn extensively as a single mom. You must be patient to parent effectively. If you don't use patience consistently, it can weaken your relationship with your child. As Kao Kalia Yang shared, "Patience is the road to wisdom." Edmund Burke said, "Patience will achieve more than force."

If you want to be more patient, you could:

- Stay in the slow grocery store check-out line, breathing deeply and imagining what it would be like for you to ring up groceries for hours a day, deal with frustrated customers and try to find the prices on items that don't have a scanning code on the packaging.
- Volunteer to chaperon on a school trip your child's class goes on. Observe how other kids are learning to be kind, share, be more patient, etc. with each other, informing

yourself that it's not only your child who may struggle in one or more of these areas.
- Schedule time to make telephone calls that could become tense (e.g., breakup announcement, performance review discussion, late payment)
- Meditate for 10 minutes in the morning and again for 10 minutes at night
- Slowly count to 15 when you start feeling tense or agitated
- Be still before you head into the kitchen to grab something you want to eat or drink. Pause.

As you're patient with your child you might notice that your child is starting to treat his friends and you with increased patience. Do these sound familiar? Have you experienced any of these situations with your child?

- You tell your child to make their bed and put their toys away before they go outside to play. An hour later, you hear your child laughing and having fun playing outside with friends. Then, you enter your child's room and stare at your child's unmade bed and nearly fall when you turn to exit the room. Without another thought, you hurry outside, yell for your child, grab your child by the shirt collar and yank them inside, hollering at them, accusing them of not doing what they were told.
- Family is visiting and you're chatting in the living room. As you settle into a comfortable conversation with relatives, your child burst into the room crying. Without asking your child why they are crying, you order your child to be silent. Your child keeps crying which angers

you and elicits the response of you leaping off the sofa and shaking your finger at your child, ordering them to be silent.

- During a drive to a park, your child keeps asking the same question over and over. Several minutes into the repetition you tell your child to sit back and play a video game rather than being patient and working to find another productive way to engage your child and help them shift away from focusing on the question that you've already answered three or more times.

Forgive yourself if you've been impatient. Love yourself. Love your child. You can't go back and redo the past. What you can do is implement strategies to become more patient.

Fortunately, life in this world offers countless opportunities to become more patient. See irritating situations as the opportunity to grow in patience. Pause. Breathe. Tell yourself that being more patient will help you. Then, seize that opportunity to become more patient instead of irritated.

Self-awareness can keep you from treating your child with impatience. Practicing awareness can keep you from yelling at your child or punishing your child because you're feeling overwhelmed.

Learn from each instance of impatience. Commit to becoming more patient. Keep implementing "patience" strategies.

You may find it helpful to think about specific situations from your own childhood where you wish that your parents had been more patient with you. But don't stop there. Think about how you would have reacted to future situations differently, better, if your parents had been more patient.

"There's a strength in happiness that can't be found anywhere else."

Chapter 13 – Growing Up Happy

When was the last time you had a blast, a ton of fun? If you grew up in a loving, supportive home, you might have a host of memories that allow you to easily recall instances when you felt happiness.

Even if you didn't grow up in a supportive, loving home, there were likely times when you felt happy. You might have been riding bikes with friends. You might have been swimming at the community pool, fishing at a lake, skateboarding or playing at a park.

Remember how good it felt to feel so happy that you didn't know what time it was or even care? During that instance, you might have forgotten a concern you had.

Didn't that feel empowering? Didn't those times make you feel strong, alive, free – good?

You have the power to gift your child with experiences of growing up in an environment that encourages and celebrates happiness. This chapter shares tips and strategies that you could use to create that very environment for your child.

Play is a Great Teacher

Your child and you will learn so much when you play together. For instance, you'll learn a lot about your child as you watch your child play. You'll notice what your child gravitates toward and pulls away from. Watching your child with other kids gives you the chance to observe your child's communication and social skills.

Not only can you use play to learn while connecting with your child; you can learn a lot while playing with adult friends. It's why so many organizations incorporate play into team building events.

Here are examples of how you could use play to teach your child. This teaching could focus on academics, communication or physical, mental, or emotional health.

- Enjoy watching math, English, science, etc. academic-based videos that use games to teach.

- Design an obstacle course. Hide questions in each obstacle. As you and your child answer the questions, move forward through the course.
- Write lyrics and sing songs about historical figures (e.g., inventors, musicians, educators).
- Complete a color by numbers pictures book.
- Place questions within the pages of a book. See how many questions your child and you answer correctly before you discover the answer within the book's pages.

See how many more ways you can use play to learn. Consider going with play that makes it easy for both of you to learn, not just your child.

_____

_____

_____

_____

_____

_____

_____

You Are "Mama"

You are your child's mother. As experienced as they are in raising children, your parents, grandparents, aunts, uncles, colleagues, and friends are not your child's mother.

Now is a perfect time to check-in on your parental confidence. If you're struggling to be confident as a parent, there are steps you can take to build confidence. For example, you could read books that focus on strengthening confidence. Additionally, you could write down challenges you've overcome and smart decisions you've made.

Reading scriptures like Genesis 1:31, meditating, counting blessings and saying "Thank you" when someone compliments you (instead of turning away from compliments) are other ways to strengthen your confidence. Trying new activities and taking on new projects at work and in the community are other ways to strengthen your confidence.

Why bring up confidence? Because if your confidence is low, you could let someone else tell you how to raise your child. This involves more than accepting advice from someone you trust.

Instead, this is when you accept nearly every recommendation, suggestion, etc. that someone gives you about how you should raise your child. Areas the recommendations could focus on include what you should feed your child, what time you should put your child to bed, how long your child should nap, what types of shoes your child should wear and where you should shop for your child's clothes.

I dealt with these situations while I was raising my son as a single mom. Even with confidence, there were times when I thought another person knew better than I did how I should raise my child. Fortunately, I exercised enough courage to go with my instincts and my own mind when it came to parenting my son. Over the years, I also incorporated sound advice and suggestions I received from people I trusted.

After all, no parent knows everything. It's good to seek input and feedback. And it's good to put good advice and great recommendations to use.

Just ensure that you're the one who's raising your child. There may be times when you must lovingly tell your parent, grandparent, or a friend that although you appreciate their suggestion, you're going to try a different approach with your child.

As your confidence grows and you see your parenting skills yielding good results, don't be surprised if you're less bothered when someone gives you parenting advice. Confidence not only allows you to be your child's mother, but confidence also allows you to give others room to express themselves without you feeling threatened or getting upset.

Another benefit gained from being your child's mother is that your child will notice what you're doing. Your child will see that you are, indeed, parenting them.

More About Time Out

Worldly demands require that you put yourself on timeout. That's right. Timeout doesn't only benefit your child, helping your child to get re-centered and to focus. Taking a timeout benefits you.

An adult time-out could steer you away from burnout. That's a blessing. After all, burnout and overwhelm can lead into depression, mental imbalance, brain fog, and confusion. If you're overwhelmed for an extended period, your cortisol could increase and your parenting skills could also become ineffective.

An effect of extended overwhelm is that you might stop listening to your child. Sure. You'd hear your child's voice or see your child's sign language, but you wouldn't really "listen" to what your child was saying to you.

Every area of your life would be impacted. Work, romantic relationships, family relationships, your mood, energy – everything. So, take a time out at least once a day. Ensure you get a longer time out once a week.

This might take consistent effort if you're in the habit of aligning your worth with how long or how hard you work. Keep at it. The payoff is significant.

Start slow if you deal with workaholism. Instead of taking a time out for half an hour a day, start by taking a 10-to-15-minute breather a day. This means that you don't do any work (of any type) for 10 to 15 minutes. You could spend the time sitting on the front stoop or back porch or maybe you chill on the sofa while your kids are playing on the floor in front of you.

Progress to an hour a day of rest. Commit to doing this. Your mental, emotional, and physical health will thank you.

Precious Memories

Years from now, when you look back, you'll smile at the memories that your child and you created. Depending on what lies ahead, memories that you create can offer hope, solace, and joy.

Memories are precious, but only if you live with the intent to make them that way. In addition to being precious, memories are powerful.

If you've suffered a trauma, you know how powerful memories are. Revisit painful memories and you'll feel an instant sting. Return to good memories and you'll be greeted with joy.

Throughout the coming days and years, gift your child and yourself with the wonder and the power of good memories. Fun and play, adult time-outs, fully listening to your child and exploring the great outdoors, museums, the arts, athletic events, etc. are ways to create precious memories.

Consider your memories about a great-grandparent, grandparent or another loved one who has transitioned. Do you feel peace and comfort when you look at their pictures and recall the sweetest memories that you made together?

Once your child reaches adulthood, there's a good chance that you won't see your child as much as you did when he was in secondary school. Memories can offer you strength, bringing a smile to your face and joy to your heart as distance becomes part of your adult child and your lives.

Capture memories with digital pictures, audio, video, print picture books and journal entries. Use the space below to start capturing memories.

_____

_____

_____

_____

_____

_____

_____

_____

_____

_____

_____

_____

_____

"Effective parenting creates a bond that deepens, expands, prepares for a healthy letting go."

Chapter 14 – Letting Go

Congratulations! You have done a wonderful job! You gave birth to a beautiful child, and you've parented your child into independence.

The days when your child needed you to carry them on your hip or push them in a stroller are in the past -- evolved into memories. No more car seats. Gone are the days when you'll hold your child's small hand as you make your way down a sidewalk.

Depending on your child's age, you might be at the stage where you see or hear your child bouncing a ball, sketching characters in an art book, playing video games, or laughing with friends what seems like all-the-time. Or you might be at the stage where the sound of your child bouncing a basketball, tossing a baseball against the refrigerator door, playing their favorite song loud and repeatedly or talking on the phone with a friend at your home every day is over.

Should your child be a toddler or an infant, this may sound strange. However, whether you realize it or not, if you're parenting with love, confidence, and care, you're letting go.

Letting go is healthy. After all, the aim is to parent your child into a healthy, love-filled adult. On the other hand, if you've been clenching your child's life, unwilling to let your child grow up independently, without constantly needing to check-in with you before they make a decision, it's time to start letting go.

Letting go doesn't mean that you're giving your child up. No. You will always be your child's mother. If you're a loving mom, your child will come back to you again and again, for visits and maybe even overnight stays during holidays.

Letting go means that you give your child more and more room to bloom, to become who they truly are. This means that you start to step back and let your child pick out their own clothes, prepare their own meal, do chores around the house, and make decisions without seeking your guidance. It means that you give your child the space to move closer to adulthood.

Growing into Independence

As young as two years old, your child might start to exhibit signs that they are ready to become more independent. When you ask your daughter to come with you, she might boldly tell you, "No!" asserting her independence.

Ask your son to help you bake a batch of cookies and he might fold his arms, turn, and run out of the kitchen, shouting, "No!"

It's time to wave good-bye to the days when your child followed you everywhere, wrapped his fingers around one of your fingers and went along with all your wishes, as if he didn't have a mind of his own.

Sure. Your child will continue to accompany you wherever you go, but they may occasionally push back. More than getting older, your child is growing into independence. As upsetting as it might be for you, independence is healthy. In fact, it's a developmental milestone. One way to gain the most from this shift is to encourage your child to be independent.[19]

Independence is evidence that you gifted your child with the "belief that they are competent and capable of taking care of themselves," shared *Psychology Today*.[20] You let your child make decisions because you trust your child. Intrinsic motivation is high on your list.

Intrinsic motivation was at the top of my incentive list, but that doesn't mean I didn't stumble. I did and despite the fact that my son, Gregory, was easy to parent. For me, he was a dream. However, I struggled with parenting when he turned seven years old. I kept telling him to, "Stop getting fresh with me."

Another statement I repeated was, "Stop talking back." Then, I'd tell my son how my father would have disciplined me in no-time-flat if I talked fresh with him.

My son asserted that he wasn't being disrespectful. He told me that he was merely sharing his thoughts and opinions.

It took weeks for me to allow this fact to bubble to the surface in my mind. My son was growing up and becoming independent. He wasn't getting fresh or being disrespectful.

Soon I apologized to my son for accusing him of being disrespectful when it was me who had the issue. Not once in his life did my son disrespect me. He never even raised his voice to me.

Accepting that my son was growing up set both of us free. Instead of feeling challenged by my son's independent opinions, I listened more fully when he spoke.

When your child expresses their opinion, be encouraged to listen. There's a lot you can learn from your child.

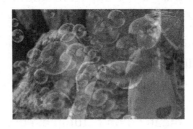

Decision Makers

At some point, the "perfect" time to let your child make their own decisions is going to arrive. Make this time easy on yourself. Revisit what it felt like when you were a kid making decisions on your own.

How did you feel? Did seconds of uncertainty pass before you opened your mouth and shared your decision with your siblings, friends, or parents? Did you wish that just one other person would agree with your decision, or did you feel confident in your decision to the point that you didn't even wonder if anyone would disagree with what you had decided to do?

When you were a kid, were you celebrated for making an independent decision or did your peers, siblings or parents laugh at you? Did someone tell you to fall in line and go along with a decision they had made? What did that feel like?

Let yourself go back, feel the emotions you felt when you made your first independent decisions. Feel what it was like as others responded to what you had decided.

Similar to how recalling what it feels like to have an aching tooth as an adult can help you understand the pain your child experiences when they are teething, revisiting what it felt like when you made an early decision by yourself can help you understand what your child is feeling when they make early independent decisions.

Support your child's decision-making efforts. Offer guidance, share comparable experiences to give your child insight, and step back and let your child start making independent decisions. It's part of growing up.

Being There

The "toughest" kid in the world needs parental support. Therefore, allow your child to become increasingly independent but be there. It may take a few tries and courage but start to step back and watch your child navigate their way through the world, offering guidance and insights as needed.

Regarding insights, little tops sharing experiences you had as a kid with your child, experiences that are similar to what your child is going through. It creates a bond. Your child may feel as if they know you better each time you share such an experience. However, avoid sharing a similar experience each time your child confides in you. But when it's best, share.

Also, be there for your child without entering "drill sergeant" mode. Allow your child to make mistakes, forward steps, and backward steps. Avoid seeing your child's explorations and attempts in a world of change as a form of competition.

Don't compare your child's attempts at learning, athletics, the arts, social interactions, etc. with another child's or anyone else's. Remember your child is unique. There is no one else in the world (not even you) who is just like your child.

Be supportive and loving, not relentless. If you grew up being pushed to "outcompete" or "outperform" others, consider bringing a non-competitive friend with you to your child's school, athletic, arts, science, etc. performances.

Listen to this non-competitive friend when they suggest that you "calm down" when you start shouting at a coach, teacher, another child, someone else's parent, or your own child when your child gets hit with a foul or another penalty, increasing the likelihood that your child won't end up in first place.

Make watching your child enjoying participating in an event and learning from the experience priority, not your child coming in first place. Also avoid making "perfection" the goal. Instead, celebrate small successes your child experiences. It might help to revisit your childhood, recalling the mistakes and awkward learning experiences you had.

Happy Kids

It feels good to thrive! There doesn't need to be a witness watching you. No one needs to know what you achieved. You celebrate by yourself, feeling your triumph.

Perhaps that's when real success occurs. When you don't need anyone to cheer you on. You fuel yourself with belief in the good you know you can do, realize you're in the process of achieving. Then, you celebrate.

Progressing -- taking forward strides -- makes you happy. It also makes kids happy.

Give your child opportunities to make small and great achievements on their own. Then, watch your child celebrate their achievements, even if they celebrate inwardly, with no more than a huge smile. Let what they've done soak into their being.

Experiences like this will build your child's confidence, trust, and courage. Each time your child explores and achieves on their own, it fuels them to try again and again. As you help steer your child away from seeing achievement or progress in a competitive way, the successes that your child explores and creates for herself may find her looking into the face of happiness.

As you watch this happen, you may start to see how your own successes gift you with happiness. If you haven't noticed, parenting is not just for your child as it regards learning, loving, trusting, and entering deeper states of joy. It's also for you.

"Thrive! It's what you were created to do!"

Chapter 15 – Thrive

Thriving is not only for your child. To single parent effectively, you need to thrive. This means that you don't make everything you do about your child. That's right. To thrive, you need to carve out a life of your own – for you.

Even if you're up for this, it might feel hard. You've spent months, maybe years, designing your life around your child. It wouldn't be a shock if you now believe that your sole purpose in this world is to parent your child.

This approach might work when your child is young. Once your child nears adulthood, this will change. If you're not careful, you could experience fear, almost as if you're about to lose a huge part of your identity, after your child enters mid-teens.

Believe it or not, thriving in your own life can protect you from clinging to your child, falling into the temptation of telling your child what to do (even after your child is an adult living in a home of their own) and feeling as if your life ends when your child leaves home.

Is there a hobby, sport, social endeavor, or nature initiative that you love? Do you think it's linked to your purpose in this world?

Revisit what's been calling to you, perhaps since you were a kid yourself. Is there a way that this calling could be linked to your purpose?

There's a quick way to find out. Start engaging in the activity. If it's the arts, start painting, sculpting, dancing, singing, or writing. Pay attention to what surfaces from within you.

Get involved in that social or nature endeavor. Pray for guidance regarding what you should do next.

Being a great mom doesn't mean that you can't have a life separate from your child's. Give yourself permission to thrive, to really thrive, doing what you love – what you came here to do.

Next Steps

We're nearing the close of <u>Thriving as a Single Mom While Raising Happy Kids</u>, and, similarly, there will come a point when you near the end of parenting. That's not to say that you won't always be involved in your child's life. You will.

But you must start creating a life that offers you room to thrive beyond parenting. In the previous section, we touched on thriving as a person vs. as a parent.

Should there be instances when you feel overwhelmed with fear as you consider living beyond parenting, think about professional athletes who took smart, next steps near the end of their athletic career and moved from a thriving athletic career into business, science, the arts, etc.

Also think about professional athletes who did not transition from pro sports into a non-sports focused area. It's not pretty to watch a once renowned athlete struggle to take their life's next steps. Instead of retiring, they hold on, clinging to a former life that's gone.

Injuries, setbacks, and team loses mount, and yet, if the athlete is too scared to move forward, they get stuck. They fight to get a glorious past to return, but it doesn't.

Little, if anything, in this world returns fully to the way it once was. Fortunately, as a single mom, you can continue creating precious memories, as well as thrive, as your child grows up and flourishes as an adult.

The only way you'll know this for certain is to start taking the next steps. Start taking the next steps before your child graduates from high school. Give yourself time to adjust to the change.

Those next steps could see you taking a vacation without your adult child. Or you could encourage your child to have fun as they vacation with friends while you busy yourself refurbishing your home, enjoying nature hikes, meditating, or doing something you're passionate about.

Welcome New Changes

Go beyond taking those next steps. Welcome and celebrate changes that the steps you take bring into your life. This single action of "welcoming changes" encourages your inner self to see that you can, indeed, thrive amid change.

In addition to welcoming and celebrating changes that enter your life, welcome, and celebrate changes that your child experiences. That might include your adult child meeting someone they want to share their life with, a date or a future spouse.

The sooner you start taking next steps and welcoming and celebrating changes, the more confidence you might have in your ability to flow through shifts and turns – changes.

You may have done this at least once a year when you were a kid. If you celebrated your birthday, you probably told yourself that better experiences were coming to you in the new year. That's a great mindset to move through life in this world with.

Just because you're an adult, maybe in your 30s, 40s or 50s, doesn't mean that changes you experience from here on out will be negative. Instead of seeing change as the doorway into an unwanted experience, keep your mind open.

Start to see shifts, turns, and change as a birthday of sorts. See change as a doorway into better experiences. It makes sense. After all, as occurs with a birthday, each change can help you to awaken, mature and grow up more.

Looking for ideas on ways to welcome and celebrate change? Check this out:

- You could buy yourself balloons when change shows up in your life. This could be a job promotion, layoff, home relocation, marriage proposal, divorce decree or financial breakthrough.
- Send yourself flowers the next time change shows up.
- Treat yourself to a concert.
- Visit a friend and hang out, relaxing and doing something you both appreciate.

You're a Champion!

Single mom, you're a champion! You've taken care of your body and your emotional and mental health for months, long enough to nurture and give birth to a beautiful baby.

No amount of pain could stop you. You may have miscarried several times before giving birth and raising a child. You might be a grieving mother who has endured this world's hardest pain – saying good-bye to a child who transitioned. There are so many paths on the motherhood journey. However you got here -- you're a mom. Celebrate the loving work you have done.

Even while you were aching from giving birth to your precious baby, you started caring for your child. That may have included preparing bath basins, herbal baths, baby wrap carriers, bottles, cleaning clothes, singing to your infant, rocking your child to sleep, reading to your baby and simply being there with your child.

Now that your baby is growing up, maybe walking on her own, weaving baskets, practicing Ginga soccer, fishing, or riding her bicycle or maybe even entering college, you're taking the next steps, actions that continue to see you thriving.

Regardless of what you face, you stir up inner courage, trust life, and exercise faith. Your child has a bright future because of parenting actions you've taken. You give back to your family and society at large. Because of you, the world truly is better. You're a champion!

Empowering Single Mom Quotes

Loving single mothers are among the strongest people on earth. They often do alone what should take a crowd of people to do.

Women become single mothers for different reasons, but successful solo parenting comes thru courage, insight, patience, and commitment to love.

Single moms get stronger day-by-day. By the time her child is grown, a single mama is a tower of strength.

Single mama, you are insightful
Brilliant, Fun
Patient, Loving
Caring and Kind
You're a doctor
Entrepreneur
Travel Agent
Writer
Actress
Student
Athlete
Scientist
Educator and more
You're a child's best friend
A confidante, a proven trusted companion.
Take a bow!

One day someone may look back and see you as their guardian angel.

Your embrace soothes your child's stormy mind – just an embrace.

You have an amazing way of turning struggles and setbacks into forward opportunities.

Single mom, one day you will look up and realize just what you have done.

Journal Pages

(Use these blank pages to capture memories, events, add pictures – anything you want!)

References:

1. Can an Unborn Baby Feel Unwanted? Effects of Stress in the Womb (psychcentral.com)
2. How Your Parents' Behaviors Shape Who You Are Today (businessinsider.com)
3. Attachment Issues and Attachment Disorders in Children (helpguide.org)
4. Being a Role Model - The Promise and the PerilThe Center for Parenting Education
5. The Power of Positive Parental Attention | Child Focus (child-focus.org)
6. The Power of Positive Attention - Child Mind Institute
7. A Better Way to Develop Your Child's Confidence (berkeley.edu)
8. 14 Strategies for Building Confidence in Your Children | Psychology Today
9. When do babies start to hear? Can my baby hear my voice during pregnancy? - BBC Tiny Happy People
10. Beware Of People Around You, Science Says You'd Absorb Their Energy - LifeHack
11. Research shows connection between consistency, productivity | Nebraska Today | University of Nebraska–Lincoln (unl.edu)
12. CDC's Developmental Milestones | CDC
13. Parenting Center: Parenting Tips and Advice from WebMD
14. Why dating apps can now cost users hundreds of dollars a month (cnbc.com)
15. How to tell the kids you're getting a divorce | Relate
16. Divorce Checklist: 15 Dos and Don'ts in 2024 – Forbes Advisor
17. How To Tell Your Child You Are Dating Someone (newsweek.com)
18. 10 Of The Best Budget Templates And Tools | Clever Girl Finance
19. Growing Independence: Tips for Parents of Young Children - HealthyChildren.org
20. Parenting: Raise Independent Children | Psychology Today

Resources (Links current as of January 2024)

Delivery & Postpartum Support

- Labor Support Basics | National Partnership for Women & Families
- The role of a birth support partner | Pregnancy Birth and Baby (pregnancybirthbaby.org.au)
- Postpartum Nutrition: What to Eat After Giving Birth (whattoexpect.com)
- 5 Reasons Why You Need a Postpartum Support Network | ACOG
- Navigating pregnancy with a disability - Mayo Clinic Press
- womenshealth.va.gov/topics/maternity-care.asp

Support Groups for Moms

- National Maternal Mental Health Hotline
- Mums Delivery
- Postpartum Support International
- Mental Health America
- Single Parent Support Network
- Helping Hands for Single Moms
- Motherful
- Single Mom Strong
- Beans Talk – Supporting Single Moms - Australia
- First Ladies of Africa
- DORAH – Single Mothers Foundation
- Single Mothers Forum - Japan
- Single Moms Planet
- Life of a Single Mom
- Single Parent Advocate
- Motherhood Support Groups - The Motherhood Center

Mentors and Child Education
- Understood - For learning and thinking differences
- Find a Mentor. Search for a Local Program | Mentor (mentoring.org)
- Council for Exceptional Children
- Head Start and Early Head Start
- National Youth Leadership
- National Dissemination Center for Children with Disabilities
- Best Friends
- Safe Haven
- National Association for Gifted Children

Financial/Money Support
- Single Mothers Grant
- Affordable Housing HUB
- U.S. Department of Housing and Urban Development
- WIC - Special Supplemental Nutrition Program for Women, Infants, and Children (WIC)
- SNAP – Supplemental Nutrition Program
- Manage your household budget in Excel - Microsoft Support
- Child Care Financial Assistance Options | Childcare.gov
- 4 International Organizations Helping Single Mothers - The Borgen Project
- Top 88 Scholarships for Single Moms to Apply for in February 2024 (bold.org)
- Financial Support for Single Parents | Benefits | Information | singleparents.org.uk
- Financial Assistance Resources | Autism Speaks

General Single Mom Support

- International Parenting and Health Institute
- One Parent
- Wealthy Single Mommy
- National Child and & Maternal Health
- Parents Without Partners
- Nationwide Children's
- Organizations Designed for Families of Children with Disabilities | California MAP to Inclusion & Belonging (cainclusion.org)
- Raising Special Kids – Help and Hope for Families

"You're stronger than you think."

Read More Books- by Denise Turney

Love Pour Over Me

Portia (Denise's 1st book)

Long Walk Up

Pathways To Tremendous Success

Rosetta The Talent Show Queen

Rosetta's New Action Adventure

Design A Marvelous, Blessed Life

Spiral

Love Has Many Faces

Your Amazing Life

Awaken Blessings of Inner Love

Book Marketing That Drives Up Book Sales

Champion! Your Will to Win is Key!

Love As A Way Of Life

Heal Gorgeous: Wisdom Within You Knows The Way

Escaping Toward Freedom

Whooten Forest Mystery: Ties That Bind

Visit Denise Turney online – www.chistell.com

Made in United States
Orlando, FL
05 June 2025

61876457R00128